# Study Strategies for Early School Success

## Seven Steps to Improve Learning

by
## Sandi Sirotowitz, M.Ed.
## Leslie Davis, M.Ed.
## Harvey C. Parker, Ph.D.

Specialty Press, Inc.
Plantation, Florida
(954) 792-8100
www.addwarehouse.com

Illustrated by Richard Dimatteo
Edited by Wendy Thomson

Specialty Press, Inc.
300 Northwest 70th Avenue, Suite 102
Plantation, Florida 33317
(954) 792-8100 · (800) 233-9273
www.addwarehouse.com

Printed in the United States of America

ISBN 1-886941-55-6

# Dedication

To Taylor and Jordyn, Benny and Nick with love beyond measure;
you are the future - bright with promise.

# Acknowledgments

To Denise Rakestraw, office manager and computer guru who decoded our hen scratching and transformed it into the work it became.  Even more, we appreciate her valuable advice, support and ability to take over the everyday workings of Educational and Diagnostic Services (E.D.S.) with her usual intelligence and efficiency. Thank you.

To Tina Silver, Director of Education and Cynthia Oberle, Associate Director, for doing their jobs so professionally that we could take the time we needed to write. Thank you both—you are a great team. And fun, too!

To Bryna Lynn Siegel whose stories contributed just the creativity we wanted.  You have a wonderful and exciting future ahead of you—just keep writing!

To Wendy Thomson for painstakingly editing to turn a very rough draft into a polished work.  Thank you especially for your ideas, contributions and touches of whimsy!

To Harvey Parker, who as he has at other times over many years, motivated us to create, continue and enjoy the process.  Our admiration for you continues.

# Table of Contents

# A Note to Students

This book was written for you because it takes more than just being smart to do well in school. Successful students are organized. They manage their time well and complete homework regularly. They know how to study, and they can read with good understanding. Successful students perform well on tests because they can remember information, and they can communicate what they know to their teachers and others. The strategies in *Study Strategies for Early School Success* will help you become a more successful student.

In this book you will learn about seven study strategies.

1.  Organizational strategies will teach you steps to organize your study time, materials, and environment.

2.  Homework strategies will help you learn the seven steps necessary to do homework successfully.

3.  Reading comprehension strategies will teach you how to identify and understand the main points that teachers and authors think are important.

4.  Learning style strategies will help you become familiar with how you learn best. Memorization and attention strategies will provide you with ways to remember and pay attention better.

5.  Report writing strategies will teach you how to prepare written reports.

6.  Oral presentation strategies will help you prepare and deliver a good speech.

7.  Test taking strategies will show you how to do well on different types of tests.

After you learn a strategy, you will do activities to put it into practice. The more you use a strategy, the easier it will be for you to use on your own. Have fun learning new and better ways to succeed in school.

# A Note to Parents and Teachers

Teachers and parents understand that children learn best when they have the skills necessary to solve problems and communicate effectively with others. In this book we have collected many study strategies to help children become better at learning. While some of these strategies have come from our own experiences working with children, many have come from other educators who have shared their ideas and tips with us for this book.

The strategies in this book are being successfully taught to students in grades three through six.  They will help make the learning process easier for your students. While all students can benefit from the lessons in this book, those who will benefit the most are the ones who:

- are disorganized
- fail to complete and turn in homework assignments on time
- cannot identify important points they hear or read
- need help in writing reports and giving oral presentations
- have trouble properly preparing for and taking tests

Learning study strategies can make learning easier and faster. Students will struggle less, enjoy learning more, and will feel proud of their improved school performance.

You don't need to follow the chapters in this book in any particular order. We began with organizational strategies because teachers have told us this is often an area where many children can improve. It is our hope that teachers or parents will present all the skills in this book to students, lead students in discussions of these skills, and encourage students to do the exercises we have provided. However, it will take more than that for students to truly incorporate these strategies into their learning styles. For that, teachers will have to frequently remind students to use these strategies and try to integrate them into all subjects throughout the year. Parents will need to frequently and consistently monitor their use, offering encouragement and guidance.

To practice these strategies we have included additional forms in the back of the book that a student may reproduce for personal use. There is also an answer key on pages 131 and 132.

# Chapter 1
# Getting Organized to Succeed

We started this book with a chapter on organization because we think organization is very important for success in school.

Most students who do well have all the supplies they need to learn and work. They use notebooks and folders to store their work. They use a system to remember homework assignments. They usually have a favorite place at home to study and do homework. They keep their study place organized so that papers and books don't get lost or forgotten. They keep track of their grades and make sure important work is done first.

If you are organized you will be able to keep track of what you need to do. In this chapter we will tell you about five skills to help you stay organized. Each skill has one or more worksheets that you can complete so you can become SUPER ORGANIZED!

Organization Skills
1. Organizing your school supplies.
2. Organizing your school papers.
3. Organizing your bedroom or study area.
4. Keeping track of your grades in school.
5. Setting priorities to do your work.

Start by answering the questions on the next page to see how organized you are.

# Are You Organized?

Answer these questions to see how organized you are. See if you and your parents (and/or teacher) agree!

| Do you | Almost Always | Sometimes | Almost Never |
|---|:---:|:---:|:---:|
| 1. remember to bring paper, notebooks, pencils, books, etc. to school each day? | A | S | N |
| 2. keep your school desk or locker neat? | A | S | N |
| 3. keep things in your book bag/notebook organized? | A | S | N |
| 4. keep your work in a folder or 3-ring binder? | A | S | N |
| 5. throw out papers that are old or unimportant? | A | S | N |
| 6. save important papers in folders? | A | S | N |
| 7. have all the supplies you need for homework? | A | S | N |
| 8. use a folder to store homework that is due? | A | S | N |
| 9. keep track of your grades in each class? | A | S | N |
| 10. have enough time for homework and play? | A | S | N |
| 11. have a system for doing homework? | A | S | N |
| 12. write down your homework assignments? | A | S | N |
| 13. have a way to get homework if you are absent? | A | S | N |
| 14. know when and where you do your homework best? | A | S | N |
| 15. double-check your work? | A | S | N |
| 16. take breaks when you get tired? | A | S | N |
| 17. remember to take your homework to school? | A | S | N |
| 18. keep your room neat? | A | S | N |

Count the number of **Almost Always** responses.
My score is _____.

| | |
|---|---|
| 16-18 | Yes! My organization is superior! |
| 13-15 | OK, my organization is average, but I can do better. |
| less than 15 | Uh-oh - HELP me organize, please! |

# Get Ready! Get Set! Get Shopping!

Look over this checklist of school supplies. Put a check in the box next to the supplies you need. Then go shopping!

# School Supply Checklist

## NOTEBOOKS, etc.
- ❏ one three-ring notebook or one per subject
- ❏ spiral notebooks, one per class
- ❏ dividers with pockets, a different color for each class
- ❏ case for highlighters, pens, pencils, etc.

## ASSIGNMENT BOOKS, etc.
- ❏ student planning book
- ❏ calendar with enough empty spaces to write in
- ❏ electronic schedule and assignment keeper

## IMPORTANT BOOKS, etc.
- ❏ dictionary
- ❏ thesaurus
- ❏ up-to-date atlas
- ❏ access to an encyclopedia
- ❏ library card

## FILES, FOLDERS, AND BINDERS
- ❏ 3 X 5 or larger file box and ruled index cards
- ❏ an accordion file folder with enough pockets for each class
- ❏ crate to hold file folders for each class

## OTHER NECESSARY STUFF
- ❏ pens, pencils, colored pencils, crayons, and erasers
- ❏ pencil sharpener
- ❏ ruler
- ❏ markers
- ❏ highlighters (yellow and at least one other color)
- ❏ glue, rubber cement, tape
- ❏ scissors
- ❏ stapler and staples
- ❏ hole punch
- ❏ paper clips
- ❏ rubber bands
- ❏ correction fluid
- ❏ reinforcers for notebook paper

# Organize Your School Supplies

Did you buy your school supplies? Great! Now it is time to keep them neat and handy!

Start with your book bag (we like to "do the worst first.") Empty your book bag (but be careful to stand back so nothing that falls out bites you). Now be brave and look through what you've just dumped out.

| <u>Yes</u> | <u>No</u> | Answer the questions by checking Yes or No: |
|------|------|---|
| ____ | ____ | 1. Is anything moving or growling? Yes? Call the Humane Society. You can also reorganize what's inside: |
| ____ | ____ | • are your pens and pencils in a case or box? |
| ____ | ____ | • are your lunch snacks in their own plastic containers? |
| ____ | ____ | 2. Are there papers you've been looking for and thought were lost forever? Yes? File them where you can find them easily, and follow ORGANIZE YOUR SCHOOL PAPERS YOU NEED NOW, found on page 5. |
| ____ | ____ | 3. Are there papers you don't need to carry back and forth from school, but are taking up space in your bookbag? Yes? Separate them into piles and follow ORGANIZE YOUR OLD SCHOOL PAPERS YOU WILL NEED LATER, found on page 6. |

Tip

Choose one day every week to reorganize your bookbag or to sort papers in your notebooks or folders. This can be boring, but it is very important to get into the habit of organizing your work at least once each week. Make this promise to yourself.

**I will clean out my book bag every (circle one day):**

Sun    Mon    Tues    Wed    Thurs    Fri    Sat

# Organize Your School Papers You Need Now

You can use a 3-ring binder or folders to keep your papers organized. Read the suggestions below to help you organize the papers you need now.

## 3-Ring Binder

Use a 3-ring binder, with dividers, one per subject. Label each divider by subject name.

## Folders with Pockets

Use pocket folders. Use a different color for each subject, and write the subject on the outside.

- Use a separate pocket folder with 3-hole clasps for homework (see the illustration below). Label the inside left pocket, "TO DO" for homework papers that need to be done. Use the inside right pocket to keep an assignment agenda page or homework calendar.

- Also buy a plastic sleeve with 3-holes to put into the folder. You will put your completed homework into the sleeve to keep it neat and clean and ready to turn in.

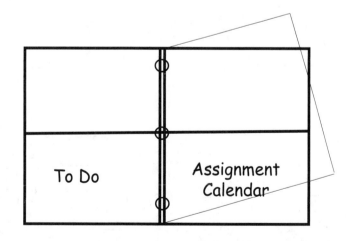

Homework Folder
2 Pockets-3 hole punched

# Organize Your Old School Papers
# You Will Need Later

There are some papers, like old tests, you will want to save to use later and some papers that you can throw away. Follow these six steps:

1. Separate your papers into two piles—TRASH and SAVE.
2. To Trash: doodlings, notes from friends, old homework papers, etc.
3. To Save: old tests with questions and answers written on them, class notes, important handouts.
4. Get manila file folders. Label them by subject and store them in a file drawer or plastic crate.
5. Write the subject, date, and page or chapter number on the top of each paper you file. When you are ready to study for a test, you will have an easy time reviewing old, but still important notes and tests.
6. It is important to get into the habit of filing your saved work every day.

**Saved Work**

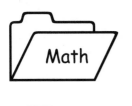

Plastic Crate for Important Papers

Garbage truck to haul away unimportant papers!

# Organizing Your Bedroom

Many kids do homework in their bedroom or they keep their school supplies in their bedroom. Check to see how neat your bedroom is. Walk into your bedroom and check the floor, the bed, your desk, bookcase, and closet. Rate from 0 (worst) to 4 (best) how neat and organized each area of your room is.

## Floor

| | **Worst** | | | | **Best** | |
|---|---|---|---|---|---|---|
| covered with papers, clothes, toys, books, etc. | 0 | 1 | 2 | 3 | 4 | really neat—nothing on the floor except my furniture |

## Bed

| | | | | | | |
|---|---|---|---|---|---|---|
| covered with books, clothes papers, computer disks | 0 | 1 | 2 | 3 | 4 | bedcovers on and clear of clutter |

## Desk

| | | | | | | |
|---|---|---|---|---|---|---|
| can't see the top because of all the clutter | 0 | 1 | 2 | 3 | 4 | only school supplies are on desk |

## Bookcase or shelves

| | | | | | | |
|---|---|---|---|---|---|---|
| things falling because they are piled up or crammed together | 0 | 1 | 2 | 3 | 4 | books, etc. arranged neatly |

## Closet

| | | | | | | |
|---|---|---|---|---|---|---|
| can't open door without something falling out or can't find anything, clothes stacked on the floor, not hung up | 0 | 1 | 2 | 3 | 4 | clothes hung up and shoes neat on floor, looks neat and organized |

Set aside one day each week to straighten up your bedroom.

**I will straighten up my bedroom every (circle one day):**

Sun   Mon   Tues   Wed   Thurs   Fri   Sat

# Picture Perfect Bedroom

Draw a picture of your bedroom *as it looks right now* or take pictures of your room and paste it on this page. Circle any clutter in your picture (on your desk, on the floor, in your closet, etc).

Draw a picture of your bedroom *after you have organized it* or take pictures of your room after it has been organized and paste the pictures on this page. Compare this neater room with the "before" picture above. Do you see a difference? Congratulations for creating the picture perfect bedroom.

# Get Energized to Organize

Some people organize every day.  They throw out things they don't need, put things away, and straighten up.  Other people organize only when the mood strikes them. Here are some tips to stay organized.

## 1. When the mood to organize strikes you—ACT!

Jamie came home from visiting her friend Sue and decided to clean the clutter in her room. She noticed how neat Sue's bedroom was. Jamie started by picking up the clothes on the floor and putting them away. She tackled her desk drawers next, filling up three wastebaskets with unwanted pens, papers, tapes, etc. Next came her closet.

Describe a time when you were in a mood to organize and tell what you did.

_____

_____

_____

_____

_____

## 2. Take advantage of opportunities to stay organized.

- When you hang up a shirt, put two or three other things away.
- When you file a school paper, check to see if other papers need to be filed.
- If you open your desk drawer to find a pen, take a moment to clean out anything from the drawer you don't need.
- Before leaving, scan your room for cups, glasses, pizza, etc. to take away.

Write some other ways to take advantage of opportunities to get organized.

_____

_____

_____

**3. Find a cleanup coach—a friend, parent, brother or sister who is willing to help you or keep you company while you organize.**

Who did you choose as a clean-up coach?_____

What ideas did your coach give you that were helpful?

_____

_____

_____

_____

**4. Do a 10-Minute Pickup.**

Set a timer for 10 minutes and pick up all the clutter in your room that you can before the timer goes off.  Challenge your brother or sister to a 10-minute pickup race to see who can clean up the most. What were you able to pick up in 10 minutes?

_____

_____

_____

_____

_____

_____

_____

# Desktop Disaster

Do you have enough space to work at your desk, or is your desk cluttered with stuff? Unclutter this disastrous desk by crossing out all the items you would <u>not</u> need for homework and study.

Think about how your desk looks at home. List the things you could put away (or throw away) and that you don't need to have on your desk.

_____

_____

_____

# Grade Tracking

Don't be surprised by grades.  Whenever you get a grade, write it on the chart like the one below.  Look over your chart every week to see where you might need to improve.

Copy the Grade Chart that you will find on the next page and hang the chart on your refrigerator or in your room.

**Quarter① 2  3  4**
**Beginning Date Sept. 2**          **Name Chris W.**

Key: T = test
Q = quiz
P = project
HW = homework

| Week | 1 | 2 | 3 | 4 | 5 | 6 | 7 | 8 | 9 | Report Card |
|---|---|---|---|---|---|---|---|---|---|---|
| Reading<br>Grade I want _A_ | T=90<br>HW=75 | | Q=84<br>HW=80 | | | | | | | |
| Science<br>Grade I want _B_ | | T=85<br>HW=80 | P=B+ | | | | | | | |
| Math<br>Grade I want _A_ | T=91<br>HW=94 | | T=80<br>HW=92 | | | | | | | |
| Spelling<br>Grade I want _A_ | T=85<br>HW=90 | T=75<br>HW=90 | T=100<br>HW=95 | | | | | | | |
| | | | | | | | | | | |

# GRADE CHART

KEY:
T = test   Q = quiz
HW= homework
P= project

| COURSE | WEEK #<br>1 | 2 | 3 | 4 | 5 | 6 | 7 | 8 | 9 | Report<br>Card<br>Grade |
|---|---|---|---|---|---|---|---|---|---|---|
| Grade I want____ | | | | | | | | | | |
| Grade I want____ | | | | | | | | | | |
| Grade I want____ | | | | | | | | | | |
| Grade I want____ | | | | | | | | | | |
| Grade I want____ | | | | | | | | | | |

This page may be copied for your personal use.

13

# Doing Your Work—1, 2, 3...

When you have a lot of things to do, decide on the order in which to do them. Check the order in which you do your homework. You can check more than one description.

___ I do the homework I like first and the homework I dislike last.

___ I do the most important homework first and the least important homework last.

___ I do what is due first.

___ I do the shortest or easiest homework first and the longest or hardest homework last.

___ I do the longest or hardest homework first and the shortest or easiest homework last.

___ I don't really have any set way I work. I do my homework in any order.


Do this exercise:

Read the following list and write each job on the "do list" called "Get It Done Today" found on the next page. Write the job in the order you would choose to do it.

—watch t.v.

—math-page 72, problems 1-15

—study for tomorrow's spelling test

—work on next week's book report

—science book-read chapter 5, questions 1-5 page 32


Have a plan:

Look at the assignments you wrote today in your homework planner. Think of which assignment you would like to do first. Write it on the "GET IT DONE TODAY" chart on the page 16.

1. write the homework on the chart in the order you will do it

2. as you complete each assignment, color in the star

3. when everything is complete you will be the brightest star

# Get It Done Today!

Date: _____

| Priority | Assignment | Color star when completed |
|----------|------------|---------------------------|
| 1. | _____ | ☆ |
| 2. | _____ | ☆ |
| 3. | _____ | ☆ |
| 4. | _____ | ☆ |
| 5. | _____ | ☆ |
| 6. | _____ | ☆ |
| 7. | _____ | ☆ |
| 8. | _____ | ☆ |

Tip

After you know how to plan, use this shortcut. Use your homework planner to prioritize your work by writing "1" next to the assignment to be done first, "2" next to the one to be done second and so forth.

# Get It Done Today!

Date: _____

| Priority | Assignment | Color star when completed |
|---|---|---|
| 1. _____ | | ☆ |
| 2. _____ | | ☆ |
| 3. _____ | | ☆ |
| 4. _____ | | ☆ |
| 5. _____ | | ☆ |
| 6. _____ | | ☆ |
| 7. _____ | | ☆ |
| 8. _____ | | ☆ |

Tip

After you know how to plan, use this shortcut. Use your homework planner to prioritize your work by writing "1" next to the assignment to be done first, "2" next to the one to be done second and so forth.

# Be the Best That You Can Be!

Read each sentence below and check the box that shows the <u>real</u> you.

|  | Almost Always | Sometimes | Almost Never |
|---|---|---|---|
| 1. I have sharpened pencils, plenty of paper, and other supplies ready to use in class. | ____ | ____ | ____ |
| 2. I raise my hand and wait for the teacher to call on me. | ____ | ____ | ____ |
| 3. I wait for free time or after class to talk with my friends. | ____ | ____ | ____ |
| 4. I pay attention in class. | ____ | ____ | ____ |
| 5. I stay in my seat in class. | ____ | ____ | ____ |
| 6. I follow directions in class. | ____ | ____ | ____ |
| 7. I finish my classwork on time. | ____ | ____ | ____ |
| 8. I turn in my homework on time | ____ | ____ | ____ |

Look over your answers. Write down any behaviors you checked "Almost Never" or "Sometimes" and choose one to improve each week.

_____

_____

_____

# Chapter 2

# Seven Steps to Homework Success

Homework experts have found that there are seven simple steps you need to follow to complete homework successfully. In this chapter we will give you some ideas and worksheets to help you learn and practice these steps.

Step 1   Write down the assignment given by the teacher and bring home the proper books and supplies.

Step 2   Choose a good time and place in which to complete your homework.

Step 3   Start each homework assignment by reading directions and following them carefully.

Step 4   Plan how to manage difficult or long-term assignments.

Step 5   Find ways to pay attention—especially when you get bored.

Step 6   Double-check your work to make certain it is accurate and complete.

Step 7   Return the homework to school and turn it in when it is due.

Start this chapter by completing the homework self-check on the next page.

# Homework Self-Check

The seven steps to homework success are written below as a checklist. Read each step and check the category ("Always or Usually", "Sometimes", or "Hardly Ever") which best describes how you do your homework.

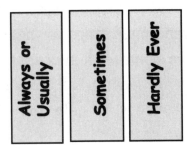

1. I write my homework assignments down every day and bring home everything I need to do my work.

2. When I can, I do my homework in the same place and at around the same time each day.

3. I start each homework assignment by first reading the directions carefully.

4. If I have a problem with an assignment, I know how to get help.

5. I know what to do to stay focused on my homework, and I take breaks when I need them.

6. I double-check my work to make sure it has been done correctly and completely.

7. Before leaving for school in the morning, I check to make sure I have my homework, and I turn it in to the teacher when it is due.

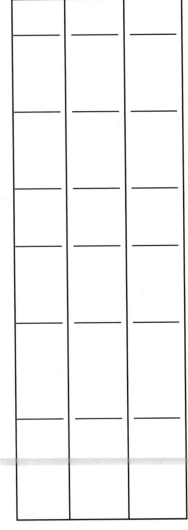

Which steps do you always or usually do?    __ __ __ __ __ __ __

Which steps do you sometimes do?    __ __ __ __ __ __ __

Which steps do you hardly ever do?    __ __ __ __ __ __ __

# Using a Homework Planner
## Today's Homework

Step 1

| Name: | | Day: | Date: |
|---|---|---|---|

| Priority | Subjects | Homework Assignments | Due | Supplies Needed |
|---|---|---|---|---|
| | Language Arts | | | |
| | Math | | | |
| | Reading | | | |
| | Spelling | | | |
| | | | | |
| | | | | |

Are all assignments copied?   Yes   No   Teacher's initials:

Suggestions for using Today's Homework chart:

1. Write down all assignments and the dates they are due.
2. Check off each supply you need to take home.
3. Before leaving class at the end of the day put all the supplies you need in your book bag.
4. Decide the order of how you plan to do the assignments. Put the number in the "Priority" column.

**Tip**

Get into the habit of using your homework planner every day. You can make copies of our planner (on the next page) or use a store-bought planner or one your school provides. Most planners are alike. They all work—if you use them.

# Monthly Planner

A monthly planner will help you keep track of important dates. Record important dates such as when tests will be given, when projects are due, field trips, etc.

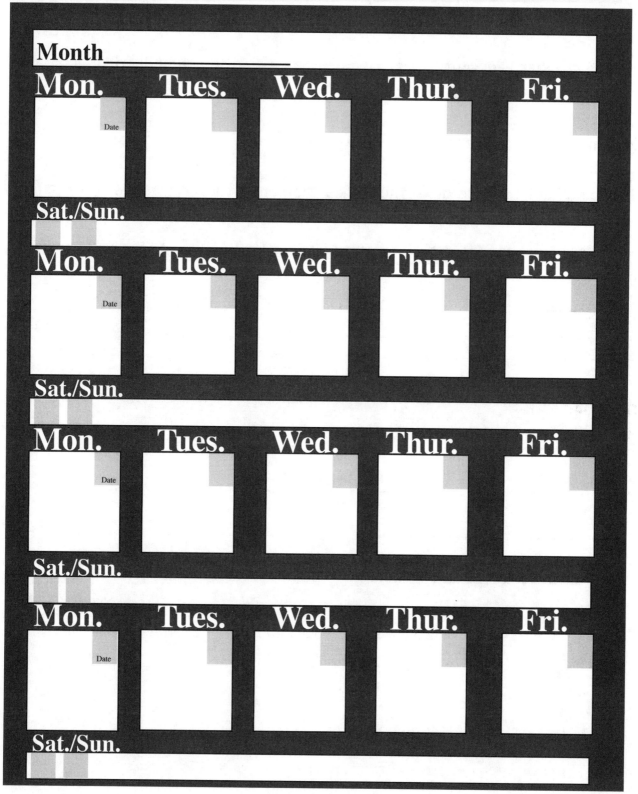

Step 1
# Getting Homework When You Are Absent

Start a Study Buddy Club!

Members give each other their phone numbers or e-mail addresses.

When a member is absent, he or she calls a name on the Study Buddy Club list to find out what is due.

Each member promises to know what went on in class and when work is due.

Use this chart to write down the names and contact information of your study buddies.

## Study Buddy Club Membership List

Names                                    Phone Numbers/e-mail

_____                    _____

_____                    _____

_____                    _____

_____                    _____

_____                    _____

Check to see if your school uses a homework hotline either by phone or internet.

Hotline phone #_____

Internet address_____

# Where, When, and How Do You Do Your Best Work?

We all have different learning styles. Some people need absolute quiet around them when they read or study. Others are not bothered by noise. Music or the television playing in the background may even help them concentrate. Some kids like to do their homework in their bedroom, either at a desk or while lying in bed. Others prefer the kitchen or family room. What works best for you?

1. In which room of your house do you prefer to do homework?

   _____

2. Do you do homework in the same place almost every day?_____

3. When is the best time for you to study or do homework?
   a. morning        b. right after school        c. after dinner

4. Do you sit at a table or desk? _____ Do you prefer to lie in bed or sit on the floor when doing homework?_____

5. Do you like it quiet when you do homework or study?_____

6. Does it distract you to have music playing or the television turned on?_____ Do you like it when there is noise in the background as you do homework or study? _____

7. Do you usually know exactly what assignments you have to do?

   _____

8. If you get tired when studying, what do you do? _____

   _____

9. If you need help, what do you do?

   _____

10. Is there anything you could think of that would help you study better?

    _____

**Step 2**

# The Learning Station™

We want to introduce you to the Learning Station™. The Learning Station™ has been developed as a system to help you organize homework tasks, work, maintain interest, and improve self-management.

The Learning Station™ is a free standing, three-sided, pegboard panel. Children place it on a desk in front of them as they complete work.

The Learning Station™ contains places in each of the three panels to hold supplies and related materials. Work to be completed is placed in a folder in the left panel and moved to a folder in the right panel when finished. The Learning Station™ also helps you practice how to break up homework time into work and break activities. After a certain amount of work is completed, the Learning Station™ is also a place where fun activities are available.

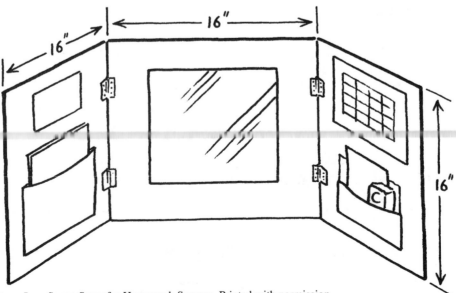

# How to Build a Learning Station™

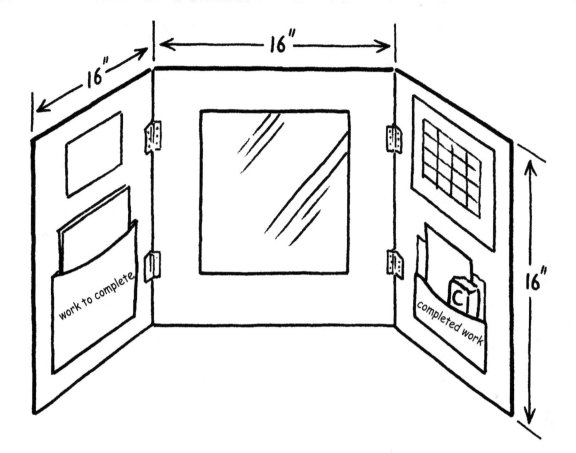

The Learning Station™ is a free standing, three sided, pegboard panel. Pegboard is sold in local hardware or lumber stores. Ask the store to cut three 16 inch square panels. The panels can be connected with small screws into hinges, two to a side, placed an equal distance from each other. If you are not mechanically inclined, the panels can be attached using strips of duct tape on front and back. Lay the three panels down on a flat surface, tape one side extending the edges of the tape over and folding them back on the next side. Turn over and repeat the process. Although not as effective as hinges, duct tape will work. The board can be spray painted with a bright color of your choice.

Step 2

# My Perfect Study Area

Draw a picture of your perfect study area.

# Homework? How, When and Where?

Find a study place at home that works best for you, but first answer these questions.

**HOW** do I like to do my homework or study?
____ alone
____ with a friend or classmate
____ with my parents nearby

**WHEN** do I like to do my homework?
____ right after school
____ after I've had a snack
____ after I've had time to play or watch TV
____ after dinner
____ after my parents get home from work

**WHERE** do I like to do my homework or study?
____ in my room
____ in another room in my house where my family is
____ in a room near where my family hangs out
____ at a desk or table
____ on my bed
____ on the floor
____ wherever_____

Now that you know how, when and where to study, it is time to get down to work.

 Tip

Make an "interruption-free rule" during the time you are studying. No video games, phone calls, t.v., or music blasting!

Step 2

# What is Your Time Schedule Like?

Do you sometimes wonder if you have time for play or after school activites and homework? Use this page to write your weekly schedule. Think of a regular school week and fill in how you spend your time each day after school. Then think about when the best time is each day to do homework.

For example:    Activities: soccer practice 2 hours; watch tv 30 min

Homework: science, 45 min; reading, 20 min.

After school:

_____

_____

When is the best time for homework today?_____

After school:

_____

_____

When is the best time for homework today?_____

After school:

_____

_____

When is the best time for homework today?_____

After school:

_____

_____

When is the best time for homework today?_____

After school:

_____

_____

When is the best time for homework today?_____

Step 3

# Direction Finder

Read directions carefully before beginning work. When you read directions it is important to pay attention to the "direction words" that tell you how to mark your answers. In the directions below underline the "direction words" that tell you how to mark your answers.

*Example:*  <u>Draw</u> a box around the right answer.

1. Circle the verb in each sentence.

2. Read each sentence and write the letter "N" if the underlined word is a noun.

3. Fill in the blank with the correct answer.

4. Copy the answer to each multiplication problem in the column to the right.

5. Find the mistake in each sentence and cross it out.

6. Shade in the circle next to the right answer.

7. Write a sentence for each spelling word on your list.

8. Select three of the five questions below and write your answers for each one.

9. On this quiz, you will need to match the word in the first column with its synonym in the second column.

10. Color all odd numbers blue. Circle all even numbers. If a number is odd and ends in the digit "3", draw a square around it.

11. Underline the misspelled word in each sentence.

Step 4
# Solutions for Common Homework Problems

Below are a few common homework problems and some solutions. Write another solution for each problem.

Problem:    I am so busy with other activities after school that I don't have time for homework.

Solution 1:  Skipping homework is not a choice. Choose one activity you won't mind skipping to make room for homework.

Solution 2: _____

Problem:    I get involved in watching television and before I realize it, I don't have enough time to do my homework.

Solution 1:  A little television self-control is needed here! Tackle your homework first, then watch t.v. as a reward. If you are afraid you'll miss an important show— tape it! Once you get into the habit of getting down to work, it will be easier.

Solution 2: _____

Problem:    I forget to take my books home or I don't write down all of the assignments.

Solution 1:  Use an assignment planner and check off the supplies you need for each subject. Before you leave school check your assignment planner again to make sure you have everything you need. Get in the habit of putting books you want to take home in your book bag right away so you won't be without them.

Solution 2: _____

Problem:    I can't get my homework done even though I spend a lot of time on it.

Solution 1:  Be careful not to fall into some homework traps—start your work right away, skip problems that you don't understand then ask for help, be careful not to daydream (this wastes time), set a time limit for each subject and try to "beat the clock." Promise yourself a reward if you finish on time.

Solution 2: _____

Problem:    I always start long projects too late and have to rush at the last minute to finish them.

Solution 1:  Use a monthly planner and break the project down into smaller parts. Set a date for each part.

Solution 2: _____

# Ask for Help When You Need It

"Why didn't you finish your math homework?" Mrs. Gordon asked Sam.
"I got stuck on problem seven and didn't know what to do." Sam replied.
"Next time ask for help!" advised his teacher.

Successful people know when to ask for help, and they are able to find others who can help them. Consider your family, friends, and others you know who you can go to for help. You may go to your mother for help in math, but your father for help in language arts.  List the names in the spaces below.

teachers

brothers or sisters

librarians

_____

_____

_____

tutors

friends

_____

parents

_____

_____

homework hotline

neighbors

_____

_____

other relatives

grand-parents

_____

_____

Step 4

# Talking With Teachers Can Be Easy

You may need to ask a teacher for help, but you need to know good ways to ask for that help. Make sure it's a good time for the teacher to talk. Be clear about what your problem is and what you are asking. Be respectful even if the teacher does not agree with you.

Read what happened to these students. Put a check in the box if anything like this has happened to you.

❑ Benny was going to be late turning in his book report even though his teacher said it had to be in on time.

❑ Taylor's teacher assigned a report topic and said, "No changes allowed." Taylor can't find enough information and wants a different topic.

❑ Nick knows he turned his homework in, but his teacher says she doesn't have it.

❑ Jordyn listens in class and does her homework, but she still "doesn't get" fractions.

Write a problem you needed or still need to discuss with your teacher. What would be a good way to ask for help?

_____

_____

_____

Tip

Teachers are usually very busy. Try to ask for help when you think the teacher may not be so busy.

Step 4
# Brainstorming When You Are Stuck on a Problem

Brainstorming is a good way to solve problems. Brainstorming is a process. Mr. Clark explained to his class the four steps in brainstorming to solve a problem.

Step 1:     Think of ideas. Any ideas will do. Don't judge anything anyone says.
Step 2:     Write the ideas down.
Step 3:     Discuss all the ideas as a group.
Step 4:     Choose the ones that seem the best.

Jimmy's dog, Diesel, would not stop barking when he left for school in the morning. Jimmy's mother asked him to think of some things she could do to help Diesel stop barking. Write down as many ideas as you can. Put one in each cloud, then choose the best one or two.

**Step 5**

# Taking Breaks So Your Brain Can Rest

If you were to climb ten flights of steps, your legs would be tired, and you would need to rest your muscles. If you study or do homework for a long time, your brain gets tired and needs to rest as well. Some signs of a tired brain are:

1. You can't pay attention as well.
2. You begin to make mistakes.
3. You get bored and can't finish your work.
4. You become irritable and impatient.
5. You work more slowly.
6. You daydream or fall asleep.

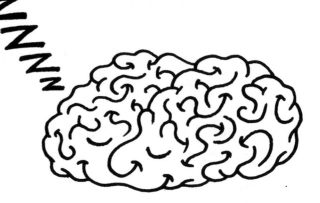

Describe what happens to you when your brain gets tired.

1._____

2._____

3._____

4._____

My 5 favorite things to do when I take a break are:

1._____

2._____

3._____

4._____

5._____

Step 5

# Roadblocks to Concentration

There are a lot of things that can block us from concentrating. Below is a list of these "roadblocks to concentration". Circle the ones that make it hard for you to concentrate. Then, write down what you can do about it.

| **Roadblocks to Concentration** | **What I can do about it!** |
|---|---|
| 1.   Music playing | _____ |
| 2.   Computer games | _____ |
| 3.   Other people | _____ |
| 4.   Kids playing outside | _____ |
| 5.   Pets | _____ |
| 6.   Television | _____ |
| 7.   Toys | _____ |
| 8.   Telephone conversations | _____ |
| 9.   People talking | _____ |
| 10.   Brother or sister | _____ |
| 11.   Tired | _____ |
| 12.   Bored | _____ |
| 13.   Hungry | _____ |
| 14.   Restless | _____ |
| 15.   Nervous | _____ |
| 16.   Frustrated | _____ |
| 17.   Confused | _____ |

Step 6

# 5 Top Reasons Why We All Make Mistakes

We all make mistakes once in a while. Mistakes can cost us time (we have to correct them). Mistakes can lead to poor grades. Mistakes can be embarrassing.

Read these reasons why people make mistakes. They are:

1. too tired

2. careless

3. bored

4. disinterested

5. not double-checking work

6. not understanding

7. distracted by other things

Circle any reasons above that cause you to make mistakes and then write five things you can do to avoid making mistakes.

1._____

2._____

3._____

4._____

5._____

Step 6

# Learning From Mistakes

Everyone makes mistakes and everyone can learn from their mistakes. The trick is not to make the same mistake twice.

Write a story about a mistake that you made that caused a problem.

_____

_____

_____

_____

_____

_____

Was the problem solved? How?

_____

_____

_____

_____

What did you learn from this mistake?

_____

_____

_____

_____

Step 6

# Proofreading Your Work

You can often catch mistakes by reading over your written work to make certain everything is correct. This is called proofreading. Read this report on comets. It contains 10 mistakes. See if you can find all 10 mistakes. Circle each mistake that you find and make the correction next to it.

## Comets

You may have seen pictures or movies of comets revolving around the sun. Nothing, however, can compare to seeing a comet with your own eyes as it glides past the sun

For many years, people were scared of comets because they didn't know what they were? We now no that they are like huge snowballs made of ice and dust that hurl through space.

Unlike snowballs that you randomly toss around with your friends, the paths of comets are predictable. the work of Sir Isaac newton and Edmond Halley allowed scientists to predict when comets, like Halley's Comet, would pass close buy our way.

The portion of the comet that we can see in the sky is actually the tale , not the body of the comet. Their are actually too types of comet tails. One is made of gas and the other of dust. The next time a comet comes passing through our skies, try to get out and view it. You wont' be sorry.

Step 6

# Double-Checking Math Work

You can avoid turning in papers that have careless mistakes if you get into the habit of double-checking your work. Find and circle the mistakes that Ann made when she turned in this math paper and correct each one.

1. 21 + 45 = 65

2. 81 X 6 = 486

3. 7 X 8 = 55

4. 17 X 5 = 95

5. 13 + 13 + 13 = 69

6. 12 - 4 = 7

7. 1/2 + 1/2 = 1

8. 1 quarter plus 3 dimes = 40 cents

9. 5 quarters plus 1 nickel plus 3 pennies = $1.23

10. 721 - 100 = 621

11. $$\begin{array}{r} 100 \\ +25 \\ \hline 125 \end{array}$$

12. $$\begin{array}{r} 234 \\ \underline{X\ 12} \\ 468 \\ \underline{2340} \\ 2{,}708 \end{array}$$

13. $$\begin{array}{r} 7213 \\ \underline{X27} \\ 50491 \\ \underline{144260} \\ 194{,}751 \end{array}$$

14. $$\begin{array}{r} 4\ 1/3 \\ \underline{+\ 6\ 2/3} \\ 11 \end{array}$$

Step 7

# But Teacher, I Did My Homework - It's At Home with My Lunch!

Do you forget to bring your homework and books to school?  Try this!
Use masking tape to divide your desk top at home into
three parts: To Do; Doing; and Done

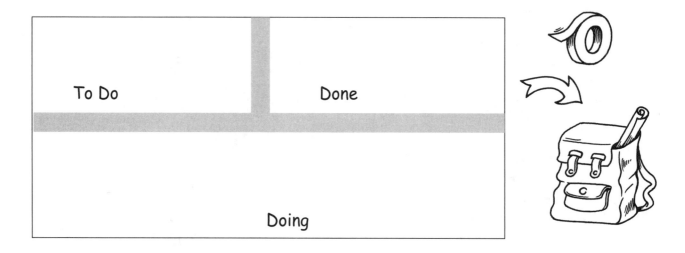

1.  Pile the books, papers, and supplies you need to use on the "To Do" area.
2.  Begin working on the first assignment in the "Doing" area. When you're done, place the papers on the "Done" area.
3.  Check your completed work, put it in your homework folder, then immediately into your book bag.
4.  Place your full book bag by the door, so it is ready for you in the morning.

Try this for a week. Put a check or star for each day you remember to bring back all your books and work.  After a week, reward yourself for great remembering.

| Mon | Tues | Wed | Thurs | Fri |
|-----|------|-----|-------|-----|
|     |      |     |       |     |

# Chapter 3
# Reading for Meaning

The ability to read with understanding is very important for school success. Much of the information we learn in school is written either in books or notes. It is very important that you have the ability to understand what you read. In this chapter you will learn five skills to improve your reading comprehension.

Reading comprehension skills.
1.  Reading for the main idea and important details.
2.  How to paraphrase.
3.  How to make a mind map.
4.  Strategies to learn new vocabulary words.
5.  Getting the most out of your textbooks.

# Picture Perfect Understanding

An author will often use a picture or an illustration to help you better understand and remember what you have read. You can tell the TOPIC, MAIN IDEA, and IMPORTANT DETAILS from pictures. Look at the picture below and circle the answers to the questions.

1.  Who or what is the story about?
    A. School
    B. Alien
    C. Textbook

2.  What does the writer tell you about the TOPIC? That is its MAIN IDEA.
    A. Schools have lots of books.
    B. Schools have principals.
    C. An alien is visiting a school

3.  What are the important details in the picture?
    A. The principal has fainted.
    B. An alien is in the school.
    C. The alien is carrying books.

# How to Paraphrase
# "The One Sentence Summary"

**Paraphrase** is just a fancy word for telling the topic, main idea, and important details about a paragraph, textbook section or chapter, or story *in your own words.*

Here is an easy way to learn how to paraphrase. Ask yourself these questions about what you've read and combine your answers into a sentence. For short reading selections this could be "a one sentence summary."

*Who/What?*
*Did what?*
*Where?*
*When?*
*Why?*

To paraphrase you must leave out information that isn't necessary to understand what is happening.

We have written this paraphrase about the alien from the picture on the previous page. You will have a chance to practice paraphrasing for the next stories.

The principal __fainted___ in school___when___ he saw an alien that scared him.

Who/What?      Did What?  Where?      When?      Why?

# More Picture Perfect Understanding

Look at the picture below and answer the questions.

1. Who or what is the picture about? (TOPIC)

   _____

   _____

   _____

   _____

2. What does the picture tell you about the TOPIC? (MAIN IDEA)

   _____

   _____

   _____

   _____

3. What are the important details in the picture?

   _____

   _____

   _____

   _____

4. Can you put the topic, main idea and details in a sentence in your own words? (PARAPHRASING)

_____

_____

_____

_____

Look at the picture below and answer the questions.

1. Who or what is the picture about?  (TOPIC)

_____

_____

_____

2. What does the picture tell you about the TOPIC? (MAIN IDEA)

_____

_____

_____

3. What are the important details in the picture?

_____

_____

_____

4.  Now, in your own words, write the topic, main idea and details in a sentence.
   (PARAPHRASE)

_____

_____

_____

Now read this story about Sally's bathroom and fill out the information just as you did from the pictures.

## Sally's Bathroom

Sally has a very special bathroom. She loves the ocean, so the bathroom is decorated in an ocean theme. The tiles are aqua blue and have swirls of white in them, like waves. The shower curtain is clear, with seaweed painted along the bottom and tropical plants stemming from within the green weeds. The mats on the floor are pale yellow, with pictures of orange and pink shells sewn on them. On the glass mirror are decals of sea horses, and the blinds on the window are the natural color of sand. The only thing missing is a school of fish swimming in the bathtub.

1. Who or what is the story about? (TOPIC)

_____
_____
_____
_____
_____

2. What does the author tell you about the TOPIC? (MAIN IDEA)

_____
_____
_____
_____
_____

3. What are the important details in the story?

_____
_____
_____
_____
_____

4. Now, in your own words, write the topic, main idea and details in a sentence. (PARAPHRASE)

_____
_____
_____

Now read this story about dangerous dragons and fill out the information just as you did from the pictures.

---

**Dangerous Dragons**

Do you think dragons are real? Long ago, most people did believe that huge dragons existed. They told stories of knights having to fight to save frightened girls, or "damsels in distress", from being harmed by fire-breathing dragons. They said dragons lived in caves or deep in the sea. These may be fun stories, but we have no proof that there ever lived such fabulous beasts as dragons.

---

1. Who or what is the story about? (TOPIC)

_____
_____
_____
_____
_____
_____

2. What does the author tell you about the TOPIC? (MAIN IDEA)

_____
_____
_____
_____
_____
_____

3. What are the important details in the story?

_____
_____
_____
_____
_____

4. Now, in your own words, write the topic, main idea and details in a sentence. (PARAPHRASE)

_____
_____
_____
_____

Now read this story about one man's adventure and fill out the information just as you did from the pictures.

One Man's Adventure

A man was shipwrecked on a strange island. He awoke to find himself tied down with tiny pieces of rope and surrounded by people only six inches tall. The tiny people, called Lilliputians, tied him up because his huge size scared them. On their island the man was a giant. Then the man traveled to another place called Brobdingnag where even the children were much taller than the man. Luckily, this man was only the fictional main character in a famous book, titled *Gulliver's Travels* by Jonathon Swift.

1. Who or what is the story about? (TOPIC)

_____
_____
_____
_____
_____

2. What does the author tell you about the TOPIC? (MAIN IDEA)

_____
_____
_____
_____
_____

3. What are the important details in the story?

_____
_____
_____
_____

4. Now, in your own words, write the topic, main idea and details in a sentence. (PARAPHRASE)

_____
_____
_____
_____

# Showers of Understanding

Picturing an umbrella in your mind is another good way to understand what you have read.

# TOPIC OR TITLE
## Main Idea

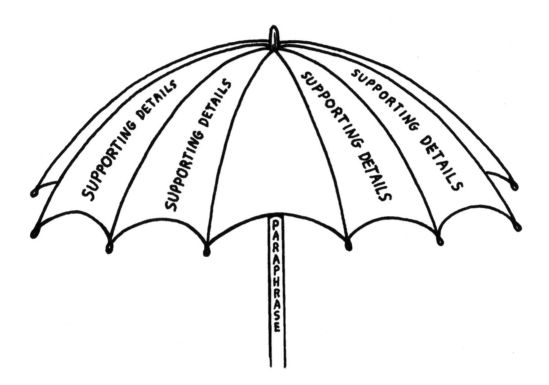

1. Picture an umbrella. The topic is the center of the top. You should be able to tell the topic in only one or two words.

2. The main idea covers the whole umbrella, just as it covers the whole paragraph.

3. The important details are the ribs that support the umbrella just as they support the main idea. Without support, both the umbrella and the main idea fall apart.

4. Finally, *get a handle* on the whole paragraph by paraphrasing what you have read.

Read the paragraphs on the next few pages and identify the topic, main idea and supporting details.

51

Read the paragraph and use the umbrella to fill in the topic, main idea, supporting details and paraphrase below.

My sister is a bookworm. There are books all over the floor in her room and on her desk and chair. She also has three whole bookshelves filled with every book she has read. Any time you see her, she is reading. She reads in the car, on the bus and at home. Her backpack is full of books, and not just the ones she has to read for school. At night she reads under the covers with a flashlight. She even sleeps with books in her bed!

# TOPIC OR TITLE
# Main Idea

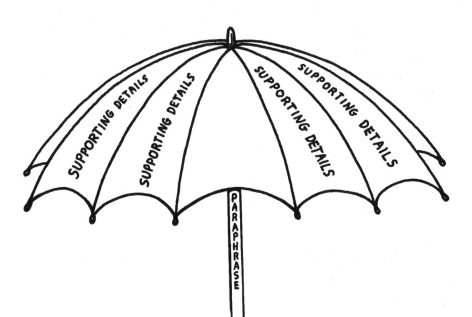

Topic or Title: _____

Main idea: _____

Supporting details: _____

_____

Paraphrase: _____

_____

_____

Read the paragraph and use the umbrella to fill in the topic, main idea, supporting details and paraphrase below.

Central Park in New York City is a wonderful place to spend a spring day. On the weekends there are a lot of people skating, roller blading, and skateboarding. Many people sit on the grass and play guitars or flutes, or listen to musicians. People also visit the Central Park Zoo, which has many types of birds and other animals.

# TOPIC OR TITLE
## Main Idea

SUPPORTING DETAILS SUPPORTING DETAILS SUPPORTING DETAILS SUPPORTING DETAILS

PARAPHRASE

Topic or Title: _____

Main idea: _____

Supporting details: _____

_____

Paraphrase: _____

_____

# Mind Mapping

You have learned how to identify topics, main ideas and supporting details. Now you are ready to use what you have learned when you read school books. Making a mind map is an easy and fun way to help you remember what you read.

Here is one simple mind map that you can use. You can create your own any way that is fun for you. Here is what you do:

1. Read your paragraph.

2. Pick out the topic, main idea and the most imporant details.

3. Put the topic/title in the middle of the page and draw a box around it.

4. Write the main idea and draw a triangle around it.

5. Write the important details and draw a design around each.

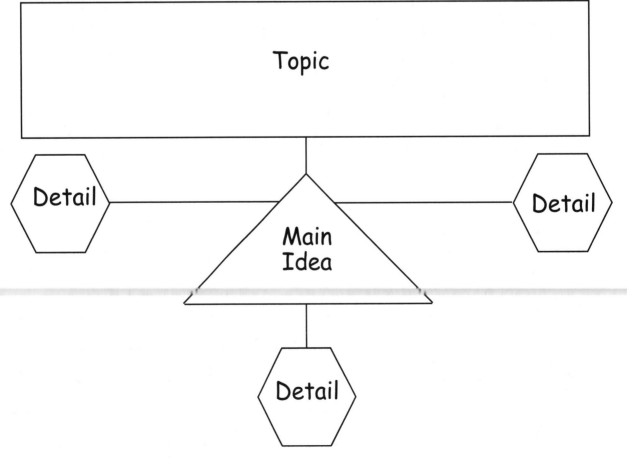

See what we did. We read the paragraph and filled in our mind map with the topic, main idea and supporting details.

A limerick is a type of poem said to have started in the town of Limerick, Ireland in the 1700s. A limerick is usually a funny poem that has five lines. The first two lines must rhyme. The last line must rhyme with the first two. The last line is usually an amusing surprise.

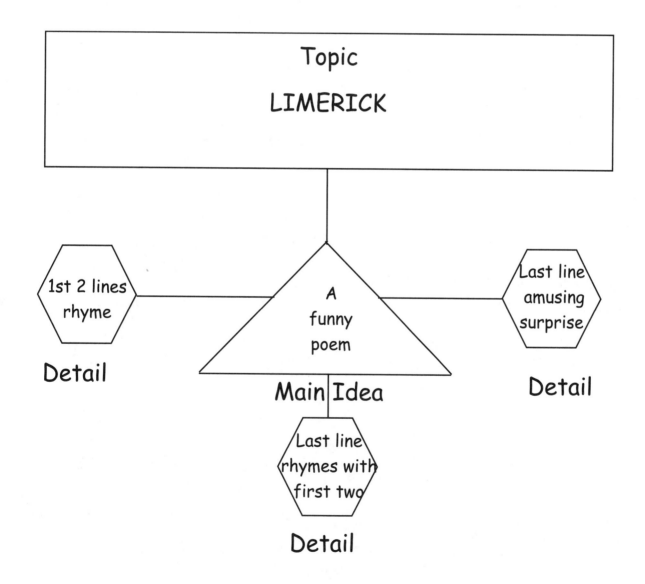

Now you try. Read the paragraph and fill in the mind map with the topic, main idea and supporting details.

Did you know that May is National Sleep Month in the U.S.A.? Everyone sleeps, but we do it in different places. Most people sleep in beds on mattresses, but not everyone. Some sleep in sleeping bags so they can see the stars. Other people, especially in Japan, like to sleep on a mat on the floor. Wherever you sleep, have a good rest.

Topic

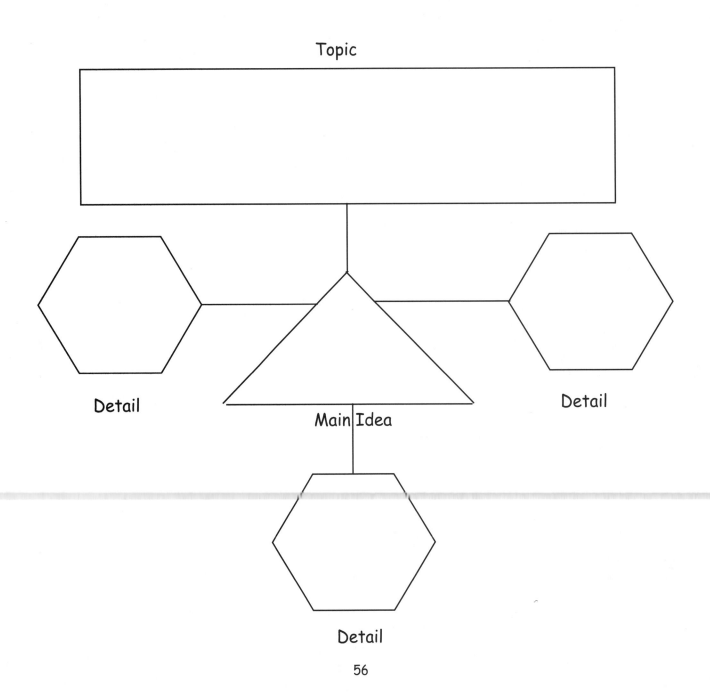

Detail

Main Idea

Detail

Detail

Now you try another one. Read the paragraph and fill in the mind map with the topic, main idea and supporting details.

When families plan to visit Florida, they often mean Disney World in Orlando. However, while Disney World is fun, Florida has much more to offer. Travel north to St. Augustine, Florida's oldest city. The Spanish explorer, Ponce de Leon, thought he had found the magical fountain of youth there, and you can still see it today. Travel west to play on the beautiful sugar-sand beaches of Florida's panhandle. Travel south to Miami and the Florida Keys to fish, swim, and meet people from many other countries. So, next time you visit Florida, remember there is more than Mickey Mouse!

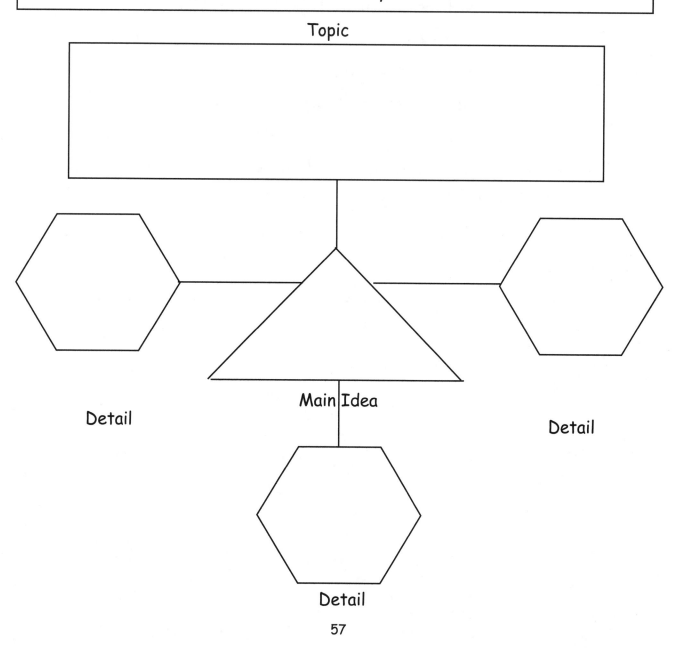

Topic

Detail

Main Idea

Detail

Detail

Betsy and Melinda are sisters who love one another, but always fight about Melinda's pet parrot, Carl. Betsy says that Carl talks all night long and wakes her up. He is also a very sloppy eater. Sometimes his food spills out of the cage, messing up the whole carpet. The worst part is that Betsy is allergic to Carl's feathers, so when he gets near her, she can't stop sneezing. Betsy tries to stay away from Carl, but Melinda often lets Carl out of his cage, which starts Betsy sneezing again.

One day, when Melinda wasn't home, things changed. As Betsy walked by the cage, she saw that Carl's claw was stuck between the metal bars. After a while, she was able to release Carl. He flew out of the cage and onto Betsy's shoulder. When Melinda came home, she was surprised to find Betsy sneezing, but happily sitting with her new friend Carl on her lap.

# Betsy and Melinda

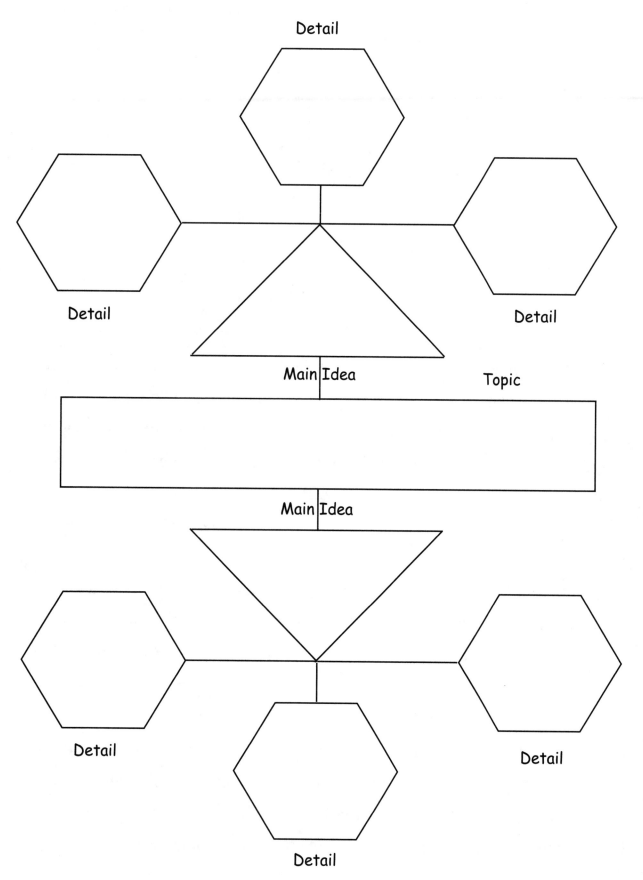

Here's another story. This one has one topic, but two paragraphs and two main ideas. Read the story about the three pigs and a wolf and fill in the mind map on the next page.

Almost everyone knows about *The Three Little Pigs* and how the big bad wolf blew their houses down. However, writer Jon Scieszka, in his book, *The True Story of the Three Little Pigs! by A. Wolf* says the story we know is wrong. In Sciescka's book, the wolf says, "The real story is about my sneezes and need to borrow a cup of sugar." The wolf claims that he never meant to kill the pigs or blow their houses down. The pigs were just not smart and the wolf just had a cold.

A. Wolf told Sciescka his side of the story. He was baking a cake and ran out of sugar. He went to his first neighbor, a "not too bright" pig who had built his house of straw. The pig didn't let him in, but the wolf did not huff and puff. Instead, "he huffed and snuffed and sneezed." That weak straw house just caved in. Wolf had the same problem at the stick house of the "little smarter but not much" brother. Finally, at the third pig's brick house, the wolf's sneezes didn't blow the house down. Instead, the third pig called the police who locked up the wolf. So, the world has only heard the pig's side of the story—until now. You can read this book to find more out about the wolf's version of what really happened.

# The Three Little Pigs

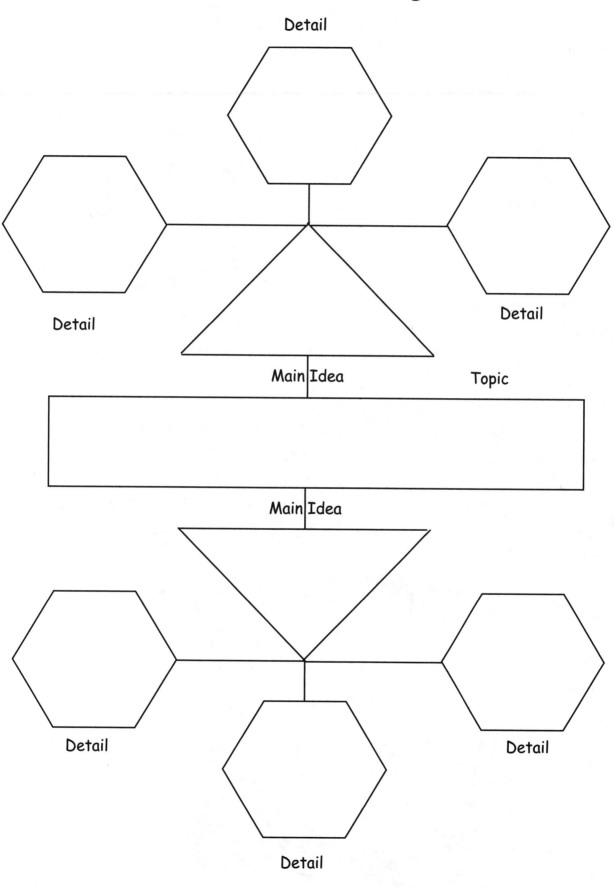

Detail

Detail

Detail

Main Idea

Topic

Main Idea

Detail

Detail

Detail

# Vocabulary 1, 2, 3, 4 ...
# 1. Sensible Stickies

Vocabulary is part of reading. You need to learn new words and their meanings for social studies, science, and even math. Here are four ways to learn vocabulary words.

Material:

> Notebook paper
> stick-to-it paper (e.g.: post-it notes)
> pencil or pen

Do it:

1. Divide a sheet of paper in half.
2. Label one half "KNOW" and the other half "DON'T KNOW".
3. Write one word you don't know the definition of on the non-sticky side of the post-it.

Write the definition on the sticky side (back).

4. Stick the words you don't know in the "DON'T KNOW" column.
5. Test yourself once a day to really learn these words.
6. Put a check on the sticky each time you get it correct.
7. When you get three checks, move the sticky note to the "KNOW" column.
8. You are a master when all your sticky notes are in the "KNOW" column.

62

# 2. Four Column Dictionary

**Materials:**

Notebook paper and binder or spiral notebook

Alphabet tabs

Pencil or pen (crayons or markers if you are feeling artistic)

**Do it:**

1. Divide paper into four columns.
2. Label each column: WORD, MEANING, SENTENCE, PERSONAL CLUE.
3. Write each word you need to learn in the WORD column.
4. Write a simple meaning of the word in the MEANING column.
5. Write a simple sentence using the word that shows you understand the meaning in the SENTENCE column (Not just "It is big" or "He is good").
6. Draw a picture that will help you remember what the word means in the PERSONAL CLUE column.

| WORD | MEANING | SENTENCE | PERSONAL CLUE |
|------|---------|----------|---------------|
|      |         |          |               |

MY DICTIONARY

| WORD | MEANING | SENTENCE | PERSONAL CLUE* |
|------|---------|----------|----------------|
|      |         |          |                |

\* A word part or picture to help you remember.

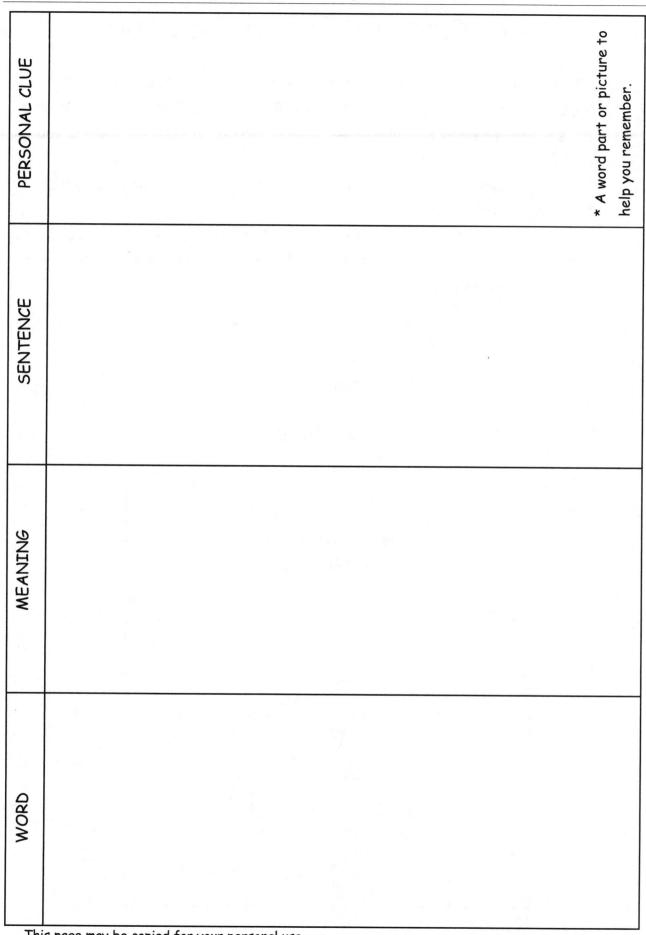

MY DICTIONARY

| WORD | MEANING | SENTENCE | PERSONAL CLUE |
|------|---------|----------|---------------|
|      |         |          | * A word part or picture to help you remember. |

# 3: Index Cards and a Picture Vocabulary

1. Use 3 x 5 index cards to write unfamiliar vocabulary words or ideas.
2. Look at the word to be learned. Is there something familiar about it? Maybe there is a smaller word within the word, or maybe it sounds like a word you know. In our example, "burden" sounds like "bird".
3. We imagine a huge bird carrying such a heavy load that the bird can barely fly because of his burden.
4. On one side of your card, write the word (BURDEN). On the other side, write the definition. Then, write a sentence that uses your association to help you understand the meaning.

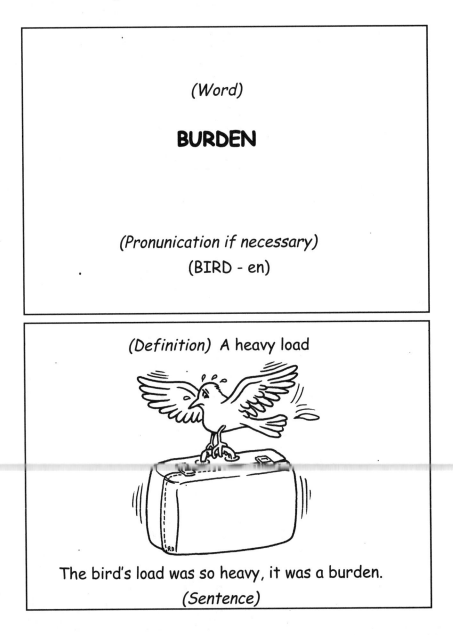

(Word)

**BURDEN**

(Pronunciation if necessary)
(BIRD - en)

(Definition)  A heavy load

The bird's load was so heavy, it was a burden.
(Sentence)

# Picture Vocabulary

Here is a vocabulary activity for you to do. Think of what each word's look or sound reminds you of and draw it. Have fun.

## Adjoining

next to; touching

## Blaze

a brilliant burst of fire; flame

## Seize

to take

# 4. The Notebook Paper Method

1. Use a spiral or notebook binder divided with alphabetical tabs.
2. Fold or draw a line down the length of the page about one-third in from the left.
3. Write the vocabulary word in the left column.
4. Write the definition and any examples or pictures to the right of the line.
5. To study, fold the right side of the page over to cover the definitions or cover the definition with a piece of paper. Leave the vocabulary word exposed.
6. Review daily. Once a week include words from previous lessons. This will help to recall meanings. Try to use words in your conversations with others.

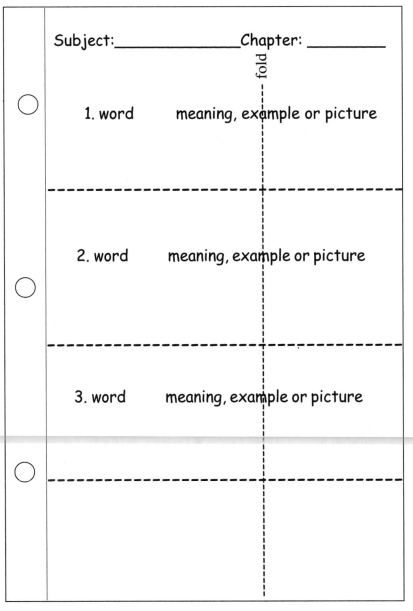

# 3 Easy Steps to Tackling Textbooks

Step 1:  Get to the meat of the matter!
Identify the facts that will be on your test.

Step 2:  Note the facts, layer by layer! Jot
down the most important facts that
will be on your test.

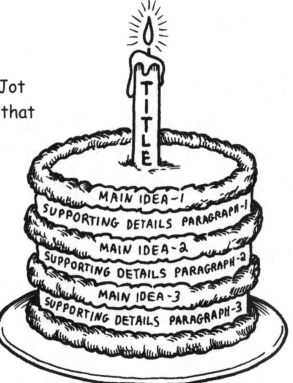

Step 3:  Get the inside scoop! Make up test questions just
like your teacher does so you have the inside scoop.

# Step 1: Get to the Meat of the Matter

Think of reading a textbook a bit like eating a hamburger. You want to get to the meat! The top part of the bun is like the INTRODUCTION to the chapter. The meat is like the INFORMATION (FACTS). The bottom part of the bun is the INQUIRY (QUESTIONS).

INTRODUCTION

INFORMATION

INQUIRY

## INTRODUCTION

- Read the chapter TITLE to identify the chapter TOPIC.
- Look at the PICTURES and CAPTIONS for clues.
- Read the INTRODUCTION for chapter OVERVIEW.

## INFORMATION

- Read the first HEADING to identify the section TOPIC.
- Read the first TWO SENTENCES of the first paragraph for the PARAGRAPH TOPIC (WHO or WHAT the paragraph is about).
- Read the REST of the paragraph for the "meat", MAIN IDEA (what the writer is telling you about the topic) and SUPPORTING DETAILS (important people, places, dates, events, and vocabulary).
- Continue the same way for each paragraph in the section.

## INQUIRY

- Answer the questions.

# Step 1: Read *Freddy the Cat.*

Follow each step on the "hamburger" to find the main ideas and supporting details of each paragraph. Highlight or underline them to use later in step 2.

---

### Freddy the Cat

When you get a new kitten, it is important to get him used to one room at a time. When I first got Freddy, he was a twelve-week-old kitten. I set up his food and water bowl in my bedroom. Then I played in there with him for a few days. Freddy immediately liked to play under my bed. I used to think he was building his own city under there. Freddy stayed in my bedroom for two weeks.

When Freddy became used to my bedroom, I began to let him out into other rooms. He loved to explore the nooks and crannies of our house. He would run and hide behind the sofa, behind the refrigerator, behind the sink in the bathroom. Kittens like to find small places where they can hide. I gave him a lot of toys so he wouldn't hide so much. His favorite thing to do, though, was watch the fish in the fish tank. He would press his nose up against the glass, like he wanted to play with fish. I had to be careful not to let him tip over the fish tank.

Freddy is a lot bigger now and still likes to do a lot. He still likes to play under the bed and hide behind the couch, and loves to cuddle with me in the morning before I go to school. But, now that he is bigger, he can't fit in a lot of the places he used to like to hide. Instead, he likes to perch on the window in the kitchen. From there he can see the squirrels and birds that play in our neighborhood. He spends many hours up there just watching the happenings on our street. He is our own neighborhood watchcat.

---

# Step 2: Note Your Facts Layer by Layer

After you read and find the main idea and supporting details, you can take quick notes that will help you study and remember. If you like cake, step 2 will be tasty for you.

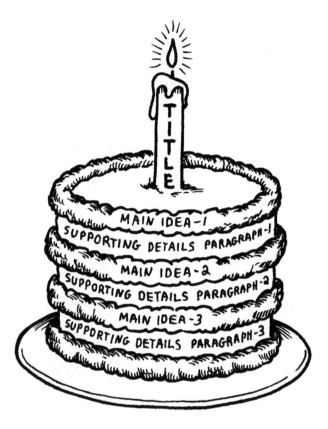

1. Think of the candle as the title of the story.

2. Think of each layer of icing as the main idea of each paragraph.

3. Think of each cake layer as the details that support the main idea.

# Step 2: Note Your Facts Layer by Layer

Look back at the facts you found in the story, *Freddy The Cat*.  Write the important facts to build your layer cake below (we like to imagine that it is chocolate).

1.  Write the title of the story.
    _____

2.  Write the main idea of paragraph #1.
    _____
    _____
    _____
    _____

3.  Write the details that support the main idea of paragraph # 1.
    SD1:_____
    SD2:_____
    SD3:_____

4.  Write the main idea of paragraph #2.

    _____
    _____

5.  Write the details that support the main idea of paragraph # 2.
    SD 1: _____
    SD 2: _____
    SD 3: _____

6.  Write the main idea of paragraph #3.

    _____
    _____

7.  Write the details that support the main idea of paragraph # 3.
    SD 1: _____
    SD 2: _____
    SD 3: _____

# Step 2: Note Your Facts Layer by Layer

Here is another way to take notes. Read the story about curling and use the hamburger to find the facts. Then, think of the cake to write your notes on the form on the next page. You may want to highlight or underline the important facts.

---

### Curling

Do you know what curling is? Most Americans did not know that curling is a sport. It doesn't sound like a sport; it's not like baseball or football. Then, in Winter 2001, curling was made an Olympic event and the whole world learned about this unusual sport. Curling has a long history. Scotland claims to have invented it. A curling stone inscribed with the date 1511 was found in Scotland. Two famous Scottish poets, Robert Burns and Walter Scott called it a "manly Scottish exercise." Scottish regiments brought curling to Canada in the early 1800s and they used cannon balls as the playing stones. In 1830, Canadians introduced curling to New England and northern Michigan in the U.S. But, curling never became an American pastime.

Curling is played in an interesting way. Curling is played on frozen ponds, streams or a sheet of ice which is sprinkled with water. Two four-person teams called rinks take turns sliding a round stone with a handle on top toward its target, or house, at the end of the ice sheet. The team with the most stones closest to its house at the end of a period wins. The Olympics got a lot of people interested in curling, so don't be surprised if a curling tournament comes to your town.

---

Look back to find the facts in the story, *Curling*. Write the important facts to build your layer cake below.

1.  Write the title of the story.

    _____

2.  Write the main idea of paragraph #1.

    _____

    _____

    _____

3.  Write the details that support the main idea of paragraph # 1.

    SD 1: _____

    SD 2: _____

    SD 3: _____

4.  Write the main idea of paragraph #2.

    _____

    _____

5.  Write the details that support the main idea of paragraph # 2.

    SD 1: _____

    SD 2: _____

    SD 3: _____

# Step 3: Get the Inside Scoop

In steps 1 and 2 you learned to find and jot down the most important facts in a story. Now you will learn how to ask questions about those facts. Why? Because when you do, you can use these questions to check how much you understand. You will also know which questions teachers put on tests. Then you will have *the inside scoop*! To practice getting the inside scoop, read the fact in each cone and match it by drawing a line to its question in each scoop of ice cream.

Winter

Harry Potter

The Grinch

Orlando Florida

To make sounds

Pucker up and blow

ICE CREAM

Why do crickets rub their wings together?

Where is Disney World?

How do you whistle?

Who played Quiddich on his broomstick?

When can blizzards happen?

What Dr. Seuss character stole Christmas?

# Step 3: Use the Inside Scoop

These are the "five W's and one How" question words that are often found in textbook study questions and on tests.

| QUESTION | ASKS ABOUT |
|---|---|
| WHO.................................People |
| WHAT................................Events |
| WHERE..............................Places |
| WHEN................................Time |
| WHY.................................Reasons |
| HOW.................................Steps |

You will now use the inside scoop by asking a 5W's and How question about the details you found.

1. Read each detail below. These are test answers.
2. Think of a question to ask about each detail. This one is done for you.

| **Heading/Title:** Freddy The Cat | |
|---|---|
| | |
| **MI:** Let cats get used to one room. <br> **SD:** Put food and water in bedroom. <br> **SD:** Played only in the bedroom. <br> **SD:** Stayed in the bedroom for 2 weeks | How did Freddy's owner get him used to the house? |
| | |
| **MI:** Freddy begins to explore <br> **SD:** He explores other rooms. <br> **SD:** He hides a lot. <br> **SD:** He finds the fish tank. | What did Freddy do when he began to explore? |
| | |
| **MI:** Freddy does a lot now. <br> **SD:** He plays all over the house. <br> **SD:** He can't fit in everywhere. <br> **SD:** He likes to perch on the window. | What does Freddy do now? |

# Step 3: Use the Inside Scoop

Remember *Curling?*
We have written the notes about curling, now you write the questions.
That is what your teachers do to make up your tests.

| Heading/Title: Curling | |
| --- | --- |
| | |
| **MI:** Curling has a long history | |
| **SD:** Goes back to 1500's. | When |
| **SD:** Scotland claims to have invented it. | Where |
| **SD:** Scottish regiments brought it to Canada. | Who |
| | |
| **MI:** Curling is played in an interesting way. | |
| **SD:** Curling is played on frozen rivers or ponds. | Where |
| **SD:** Two four-person teams are called "rinks". | What |
| **SD:** The team with most stones closest to their "house" wins. | How |

# Hey Textbooks, This is a Stickup!

After you get really good at using the 3 Steps, this "Stick-Up" activity will help you study for tests.

Directions:   Make your own study chart using ours as a guide.  You can use paper, poster board or a big piece of felt.

1.  Write facts and details you need to study on the sticky side of a sticky note. (You may substitute index cards for sticky notes.)
2.  Write your study questions on the front of the note.
3.  Stick the note on your chart under "Don't Know".
4.  Look at the questions on the first sticky note and answer them.  Check the answer side to see if you are correct.  If you are, put a check mark on the top of the note and move your sticky to the "Still Studying" column of your chart.
5.  Review the sticky every night and when you have 3 checks, move your sticky to the "Know" column.
6.  If you don't know the answer, study it and leave it in the "Don't Know" column. Review it nightly until you have 3 checks and can move your sticky to the "Know" column.

| Study Chart | | |
|---|---|---|
| Don't Know | Still Studying | Know |

# Chapter 4
# Organizing Written Reports

Can you guess what kind of schoolwork kids dislike the most?  If you guessed writing reports, you would be right.  Many kids simply don't like to write. They would rather tell you what they know.

Unfortunately, we can't avoid writing. As you go through school your teachers will require you to take notes in class, write reports, essays, or compositions.  Many students use a computer so they don't have to write as much. When you learn the keyboard, you will be able to type as fast as you can write, and your work will look neater.

This chapter will help you learn how to write book reports and reports that require research.

Report writing skills.
1. Making a chapter map for your book report.
2. Making a reading log for your book report.
3. Organizing a research report.
4. Getting the facts and putting them on paper.

# How Do You Do at Report Writing?

Ignore the rumors.  It is absolutely possible to write a report without feeling stressed.  Take this report quiz to find out how ready you are to tackle reports, then practice the strategies in this chapter to become good at writing reports. Circle either Yes or No.

| | | |
|---|---|---|
| Yes | No | 1. Would I rather clean my room than write a report? |
| Yes | No | 2. Do I have a hard time finding a book to read? |
| Yes | No | 3. Do I have a hard time knowing what the teacher wants me to do when I have to write a report? |
| Yes | No | 4. Do I wait until my parents nag and nag before I get started? |
| Yes | No | 5. Do I always need lots of help to write a report? |
| Yes | No | 6. Do I have a hard time finishing a report on time? |

Count how many

# Yes ____ # No ____

If you answered yes more than once, this chapter will help you feel more confi-dent in writing reports.

# Two Fun Plans for Book Reports:
# Chapter Maps
# and Reading Logs

In the last chapter you learned how to pull out the main information when you read. Writing reports is the next step. When you have a book report to write, it will be easier for you to remember everything if you jot down facts as you read each chapter.

Listed below are the main facts you need to remember in each chapter of the book.
1. The setting—where the story takes place.
2. The main idea.
3. The characters in the story.
4. The description of the characters.
5. The important facts told by the author.

Making and using chapter maps or reading logs can help you organize the information you need for your book report. When you finish reading a chapter, fill in the most important facts. You will find it easier to write a report or take a test about the book you have read. You may copy and use the maps and logs we included on the next pages.

These strategies are especially useful for summer reading assignments.

# Chapter Map

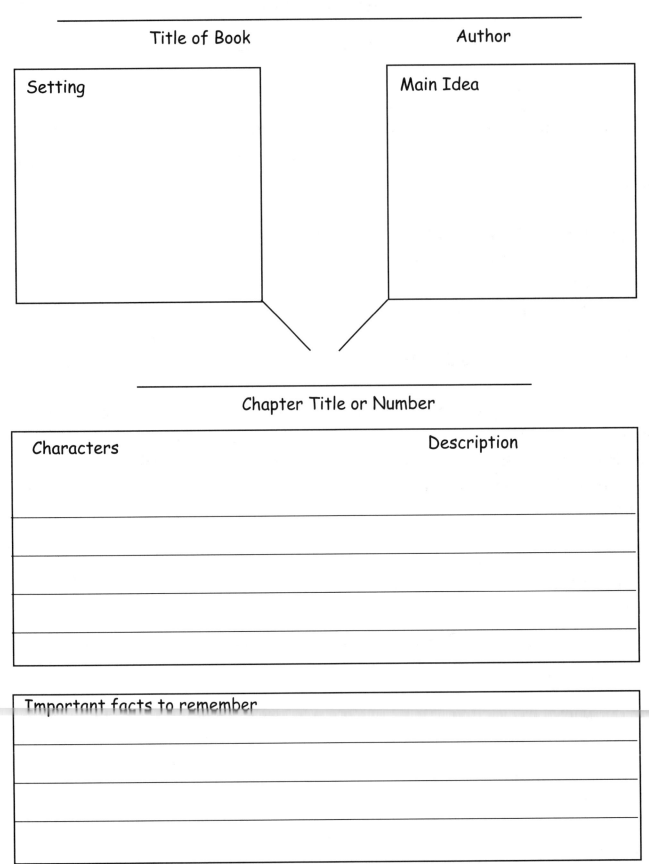

Title of Book                         Author

Setting

Main Idea

Chapter Title or Number

Characters                    Description

Important facts to remember

This page may be copied for your personal use.

# Chapter Map (Continued)

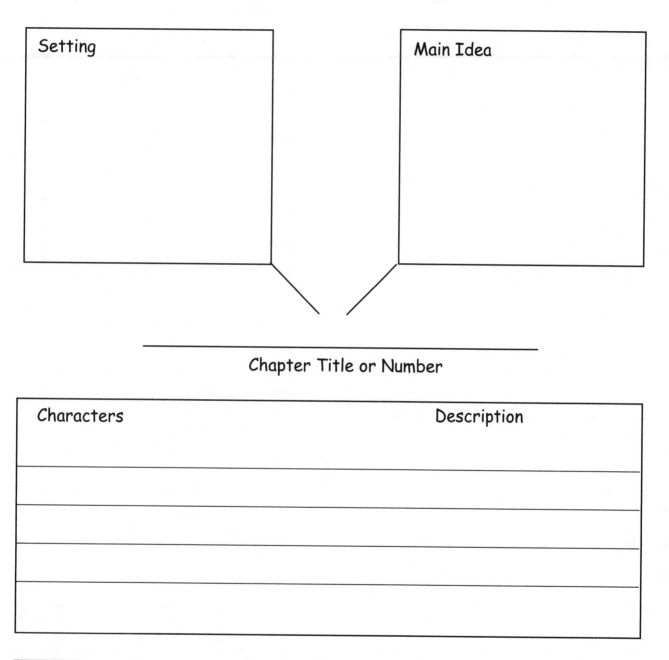

Setting

Main Idea

Chapter Title or Number

Characters                                    Description

Important facts to remember

# Chapter Map (Continued)

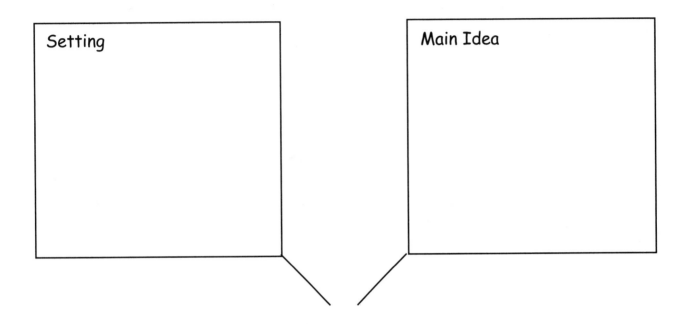

Setting

Main Idea

Chapter Title or Number

| Characters | Description |
| --- | --- |
|  |  |
|  |  |
|  |  |
|  |  |

Important Facts To Remember

# Chapter Map (Continued)

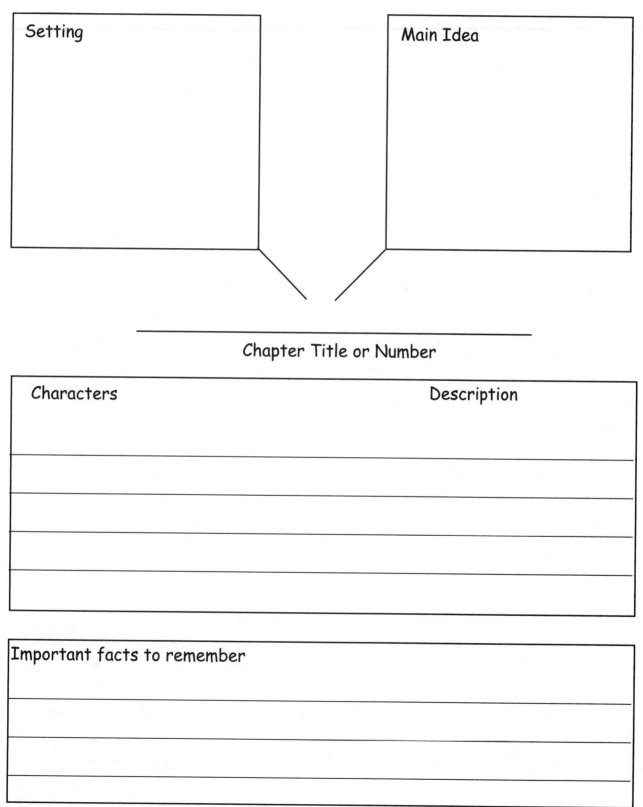

Setting

Main Idea

Chapter Title or Number

Characters

Description

Important facts to remember

# Reading Log

Title: _____

Author: _____


Chapter #: _____


Difficult vocabulary words

1. _____

2. _____

3. _____

4. _____

5. _____

6. _____

7. _____

Characters and what you want
to remember about them.

1. _____

   _____

2. _____

   _____

3. _____

   _____


Important facts to remember: _____

_____

_____

_____

_____

_____

_____

_____

# Reading Log(Continued)

Chapter #: _____

Difficult vocabulary words

1. _____

2. _____

3. _____

4. _____

5. _____

6. _____

7. _____

Characters and what you want to remember about them.

1. _____

_____

2. _____

_____

3. _____

_____

Important facts to remember: _____

_____

_____

_____

_____

_____

_____

_____

# Reading Log (Continued)

Chapter #: _____

| Difficult vocabulary words | Characters and what you want to remember about them. |
|---|---|

Difficult vocabulary words

1. _____

2. _____

3. _____

4. _____

5. _____

6. _____

7. _____

Characters and what you want to remember about them.

1. _____

_____

2. _____

_____

3. _____

_____

Important facts to remember: _____

_____

_____

_____

_____

_____

_____

_____

# A Chapter a Day Will Pave the Way

Reading a little each day when a book report is due will help you to finish the book with plenty of time to write the report. You may also enjoy the book more.

Ask yourself:
1. How many pages are in the book?
2. How many days until your report is due?
3. Then divide the number of all the pages in your book by the number of days you have left. This gives you the number of pages you need to read each day to get finished in time.

---

Example:
1. There are 100 pages in a book.
2. There are 20 days left until the book report is due.
3. 100 divided by 20 = 5 pages a day.

Now that you know it would take 5 pages a day to read the entire book, try to read six pages per day so that you can finish the book days before the report is due. This will give you time to prepare a report.

---

Tip

Remember! Reading the book is only the first step to completing a fabulous report. Leave some extra days so you have time to edit, revise and write your report.

# 7 Steps to the Finish Line

Writing a report can be fun if you plan your work correctly.  Kids sometimes put off doing a report until a day or two before it is due. The key to writing a good report is planning. To make it easy for you to get started on reports we have divided the process into seven steps. Follow each step and you will have your reports done on time.

Fill in your teacher's directions for your report.
<u>Requirements</u>

Report topic:

_____

Handwritten ❑     Typed ❑     Oral ❑

# pages _____       # minutes (if oral) _____       # sources _____

Bibliography ❑ Cover Sheet ❑   Visuals ❑

Other requirements:

_____

_____

_____

Due Date:

**Step 1: Collect Sources**
   ❑ Library
   ❑ Bookstore
   ❑ Internet
   ❑ Other _____

❑ Check this box when you are done with Step 1

## Step 2: Brainstorm

Look through your sources to find at least three major ideas about your report topic and write them down.

Major Idea 1:_____

Major Idea 2:_____

Major Idea 3:_____

❑ Check this box when you are done with Step 2

## Step 3: Big Sentence

Write one sentence that introduces your report topic and includes your major ideas.

_____

_____

❑ Check this box when you are done with Step 3

## Step 4: Fact Sheets

Use one piece of notebook paper or index cardfor each major idea.
Write the major idea on top and list the facts underneath.

| Major Idea | Major Idea | Major Idea |
|---|---|---|
| • fact | • fact | • fact |
| • fact | • fact | • fact |
| • fact | • fact | • fact |

❑ Check this box when you are done with Step 4

## Step 5: Sloppy Copy

Read your fact sheets and decide the order to use them to write the first draft of your report.  We call it a "sloppy copy".  Later you will clean it up before you turn it in.  If you hand write, skip lines. If you use a computer, double space.

❑ Check this box when you are done with Step 5

## Step 6: Edit (Clean up your sloppy copy.)

A. Ask someone to help you correct your sloppy copy.  Circle "Y" o r"N" if you:

1. wrote your own title?                                          Y      N
2. used your own words?                                       Y      N
3. used a first sentence that grabbed the reader's attention?   Y      N
4. used colorful adjectives?                                     Y      N
5. used specific nouns (and never used "thing")?              Y      N
6. began each paragraph with a topic sentence?             Y      N

7. included details in each paragraph that tell
   about that paragraph's topic?                    Y       N

B. Ask someone to make sure your report also has:

  1. correct capitals                                Y       N

  2. perfect punctuation                             Y       N

  3. sensational spelling                            Y       N

  4. verbs that stay in the same tense               Y       N

  5. sentences that vary—simple, compound,
     and complex                                     Y       N

C. Do what you need to change every "N" to a "Y" and turn your
"sloppy copy" into a "clean copy".                   ❑ Check this box
                                                     when you are done
                                                       with Step 6

**Step 7: Finish Right!**

A. Rewrite or retype your now "clean copy" and recheck it.

B. Add the bibliography, illustrations and a cover sheet.   ❑ Check this box

C. You are now ready to turn in your report.         when you are done
                                                       with Step 7

My Grade

# Chapter 5
# Giving Oral Presentations

Sometime in your life you will probably need to speak in front of a group. Whether it is simply to ask or answer a question, state your opinion or to give an oral presentation. Public speaking often makes people very nervous. However, once you learn the strategies involved in giving a speech, you can become a super public speaker, and you will actually enjoy addressing a group.

Oral presentation skills.
1. Choosing a terrific topic for your presentation.
2. Selecting sources of information.
3. Organizing your presentation.
4. Rehearsing your presentation.
5. Delivering your presentation to an audience.

# Choosing a Terrific Topic

The first step in giving an oral presentation is choosing a topic. You will want to pick a topic that you are interested in and one that you think will interest your audience. This is very important. While a good public speaker can make a boring topic interesting, it always helps to have a terrific topic to start with.

What makes a terrific topic?
• you are interested in it
• others will be interested in it
• there is plenty of information available about the topic

Mrs. Gordon asked the students in her class to prepare an oral presentation from one of the topics listed below.
1. A Diamond Worth $3 Million
2. The Biggest Snowball in the World: Glaciers in the Arctic
3. Living with Rattlesnakes
4. The Greatest President the U.S. Ever Had
5. Is There Life on Mars?
6. My Favorite Television Show
7. Comets and Our Solar System
8. What Makes America Great
9. My Favorite City in the World
10. My Favorite Sports Hero

Which one would you have chosen? Why?

_____

_____

_____

_____

# Selecting Sources of Information

When teachers assign a project such as a written or oral report, they usually like you to use different sources of information in preparing your report. This is called RESEARCH. Teachers like RESEARCH because it gives students a chance to learn how to use different reference sources.

## Selecting Sources

Below is a list of sources you can use to research a topic. Circle the ones that you have used in the past to get information.

| | | |
|---|---|---|
| encyclopedia | scientific journal | fiction titles |
| atlas | radio | textbook |
| newspaper | television | personal interviews |
| magazine | songs | internet |

## Keeping Track of Your Sources

When you find a good source, write its title and other important information (author, publisher, date published, pages) on a note card (or source card). Number each source card and write that number on the note card on which you will write the information from your sources. At the end of your speech you can give the appropriate credit to your sources.

For example:

"My sources of information for this speech were the Encyclopedia Britannica and a book by Roger Fields called, *Hamsters, Gerbils, and other Small Creatures*, by Rodent Press. "

# Organizing the Presentation

Organizing a presentation is similar to preparing a written report. We went over these steps in "7 Steps to the Finish Line" in the last chapter.

An oral presentation has three basic parts: the introduction, the body, and the conclusion.

Introduction—Tell them what you are going to tell them!

Body—Tell them!

Conclusion—Tell them what you told them!

## Introduction

The introduction is the start of your presentation. You want to grab the audience's attention and give them a reason to listen to the rest of what you have to say. To grab your audience's attention, start with a story, a quotation, a thoughtful question, an interesting picture or display.

Alex is preparing a speech on whaling. Which of these introductions would you find most interesting? Why?

• I'm going to tell you about the history of whaling.

• Did you know that whales are the largest mammals on the planet?

• You can find whales in many different oceans.

• Whales actually help people by supplying us with many different products.

## The Body

The body of the speech is usually written first. This is where you use the information you have collected from your research.

1. Go through the note cards you have made from your research.

2. Write a topic sentence to introduce your speech.

3. Write a one sentence summary for each main idea and some details.

## The Conclusion

The conclusion is like your introduction, but in reverse. Begin the conclusion with a review of the main ideas covered in the speech. A couple of sentences should do. End with a memorable statement.

# Presenting the Speech

The key to giving a great speech is practice, practice, practice!

1. Study your notecards and become familiar with the facts to present.

2. Read your written speech over and over so you have a good sense of how to connect the main ideas and details you have researched.

3. Review your notecards so that you can recite the information from the facts you have written.

4. Practice giving your speech orally. Rehearsing aloud helps you discover the phrases that sound good and gets you comfortable with expressing yourself. Go through the entire speech several times, but don't worry about memorizing every word. If you know your information, you will easily be able to speak about it.

# Tips on Practicing Your Delivery

1. Full Voice. Use your full voice when you practice. Don't just read your notecards to yourself or just above a whisper. Use a full, loud voice. Make believe your audience is sitting in front of you when you rehearse. Make sure the person all the way in the back can hear you. Speak slowly, clearly and loudly.

2. Eyes up, not down. You need to connect with your audience, not with your note cards. To do this you should look at individual people in your audience. Make eye-contact with a few of them and hold that eye contact for a second or two. Don't hold your note cards too far down. Hold them up. You should have the key points written on each note card.

   If you are using a lecturn, place the note cards on the lecturn and keep your hands free (don't grab the lecturn). Use your hands, your eyes, and your body to emphasize what you are saying. A rigid posture, fixed hands and a downward gaze will lose your audience.

3. Attract attention. Use your voice and your body to attract attention. Smile, point, move around a bit. This makes you an interesting presenter. Your audience will want to see what happens next.

4. Use technology. Use technology when you can. Record yourself giving your speech either by using a video camera or an audio tape recorder, then review it.

5. Use cues. Write messages to yourself on your notecards. "Look up." "Loud Voice." "Stay Calm."

# Chapter 6
# Learning Style, Memory, and Attention

## Your Learning Style

Some people learn best by watching. They are visual learners. Some people learn best by hearing. They are auditory learners. Others learn best by doing. We call them kinesthetic learners. Still others learn when they combine all these methods of learning. In this chapter we will help you figure out what kind of learning style suits you.

## Improving Your Memory

Memory plays an important part in school success. What if you never were able to remember the mulitiplication tables, the capitals of states, definitions of words, or important dates in history? Learning would not be of much use without remembering. We can use all of our senses to remember. We remember what we smell, what we see, and what we hear and touch. We will show you some strategies to help you remember facts.

## It Pays to Pay Attention

Of course, to learn and remember, you need to pay attention. We have included a few strategies to help improve your attention span.

Learning, memory, and attention skills.
1. Knowing your learning style.
2. Using acronyms to help you remember.
3. Making charts, pictures, and rhymes to improve memory.
4. Paying attention to your attention.

# What is Your Learning Style?

Read each statement.  Check all that describe how you would study for a big test.

HARDLY

<u>YES</u>  <u>SOMETIMES</u>  <u>EVERY</u>

**Are you a VISUAL LEARNER?** (You learn best by seeing.)

____  ____  ____  1. I read the facts over and over.

____  ____  ____  2. I write things down to see them.

____  ____  ____  3. I close my eyes to "see" things in my mind.

____  ____  ____  4. I look at pictures that show me more.

____  ____  ____  5. I use flash cards or note cards.

____  ____  ____  6. I like to read or take notes better than only listening to the teacher.

**Are you an AUDITORY LEARNER?** (You learn best by listening.)

____  ____  ____  7. I say the information over and over.

____  ____  ____  8. I ask someone to talk about the facts with me.

____  ____  ____  9. I listen to the teacher. Listening carefully helps me remember.

____  ____  ____  10. I wish I could listen to books instead of reading them.

____  ____  ____  11. I use rhymes or songs to remember.

____  ____  ____  12. I like someone to quiz me.

**Are you a KINESTHETIC learner?** (You learn best by doing)

____  ____  ____  13. I write facts down.

____  ____  ____  14. I draw pictures about the subject.

____  ____  ____  15. I move around when I study.

____  ____  ____  16. I like to be shown how to do something.

____  ____  ____  17. I like to act out or demonstrate what I know better than telling about it.

From my answers it seems that I am:

____  a visual learner

____  an auditory learner

____  a kinesthetic learner

____  a visual, auditory, and kinesthetic learner

Most people learn through a combination of these styles.

# How Do You Remember Best?

Below is a list of study secrets that some students use to help them remember. Check the ones that you use.

____  see pictures or movies in your mind

____  color code

____  use pictures, charts, maps, etc.

____  watch the teacher's facial and body cues

____  use computers and/or videos

____  use flash cards or note cards to help you remember

____  move around while you study

____  take breaks between subjects

____  color code notebooks and papers

____  use a highlighter to mark important facts

____  take notes

____  draw illustrations

____  learn by doing

____  make a diorama

____  write and illustrate a story to help you remember something

____  role play

____  listen to tapes

____  make up rhymes, songs

____  listen for teacher's verbal cues

____  be part of a study group

____  talk out loud to yourself

____  read aloud

____  have someone quiz you

____  join in class discussions

____  use a tape recorder

____  other _____

____  other _____

Look over the list again. Put a "+" by other ones you wuold like to use. Try a new study secret each time you study to decide if it will work for you.

# Silly Sentences

It is easier to remember a list if it makes sense the way a sentence does. So, think of something you need to memorize and use the first letter of each word to make a SILLY SENTENCE. The real name for your silly sentence is ACROSTIC.

Examples:
To remember the planets in their order from the sun, use this Silly Sentence:
**M**ercury **V**enus **E**arth **M**ars **J**upiter **S**aturn **U**ranus **N**eptune **P**luto
**M**y **V**ery **E**ducated **M**other **J**ust **S**erved **U**s **N**ine **P**izzas.

Math order of operations:
**P**arenthesis, **E**xponents, **M**ultiplication, **D**ivision, **A**ddition, **S**ubtraction
**P**lease **E**xcuse **M**y **D**ear **A**unt **S**ally.

Now its your turn! Make up your own SILLY SENTENCE to help you remember these:

1.  The musical notes of the treble clef: **E, G, B, D, F**
    Our Silly Sentence: **E**very **G**ood **B**oy **D**oes **F**ine.

    Your Silly Sentence:

    _____

2.  The order of doing long division: divide, multiply, subtract, bring down
    Our Silly Sentence: **D**addy **M**other **S**ister **B**rother **D**ance.

    Your Silly Sentence:

    _____

3.  The oceans of the world from largest to smallest: Pacific, Atlantic, Indian and Arctic.
    Our Silly Sentence: **P**enguins **A**te **I**ce cream in **A**ugust.

    Your Silly Sentence:

    _____

Tip
If you have a long list to study, you may need to make more than one Silly Sentence.

104

# Wacky Words

Another fun way to remember details is to use the first letter from each word you need to learn and replace it with a WACKY WORD (also called an ACRONYM). Your wacky word can be real or nonsense. Just be sure you can pronounce it.

Example:  The five U.S. Great Lakes are **H**uron, **O**ntario, **M**ichigan, **E**rie and **S**uperior.
Our Wacky Word is: **HOMES** (That is easier to remember!)
Example:  Our SILLY SENTENCE for math operations was **P**lease **E**xcuse **M**y **D**ear **A**unt **S**ally.  You can shorten that and memorize **PEMDAS** instead.

Now have fun making up even more of your own WACKY WORDS. To make your WACKY WORDS remind you of what you need to memorize, put other words with it, like "lake" **HOMES**. This is how you use a context clue.

Make a WACKY WORD to remember:
1.  The 3 bones of the ear: **H**ammer, **A**nvil and **S**tirrup.

    Your Wacky Word: _____

2.  The four constellations in the night sky: **P**egasus, **P**isces, **T**aurus, **O**rion.

    Your Wacky Word: _____

3.  The 7 continents of the world: **A**frica, **A**sia, **N**orth America, **S**outh America, **A**ustralia, **E**urope and **A**ntarctica.

    Your Wacky Word: _____

Tip

If you have a long list of details to study, make more than one Wacky Word. Remember to Keep It Simple (KIS).

# Charming Charts

When you need to compare two ideas, it is so much easier to make a chart.  Write headings and fill in the details as you find them.

When test time comes, you only need to check your chart.

Example:  To compare cloud types: Cirrus, Cumulus, and Stratus.

|  | Made of | Looks like | How close to earth |
|---|---|---|---|
| Cirrus | Mostly ice crystals | Curly white | High |
| Cumulus | Water droplets or ice | Heaps of cotton balls | Vertical high to low |
| Stratus | Water droplets or ice crystals | Layers or sheets | Low |

Here is information that you can chart.

1.  Compare baseball, football and basketball.  We've done the headings; you fill in the details.  If you need more information, look in books, on the computer, or ask your family, friends, or any professional athletes you are lucky enough to know.

|  | # of players | Quarters/Innings | Played on a ....... | Size or shape of ball |
|---|---|---|---|---|
| Baseball |  |  |  |  |
| Football |  |  |  |  |
| Basketball |  |  |  |  |

2. Compare types of transportation.  This time you fill in the headings.

|  |  |  |  |  |
|---|---|---|---|---|
| Plane |  |  |  |  |
| Train |  |  |  |  |
| Boat |  |  |  |  |

3. Draw your own chart below to fill in details to compare any three relatives (such as your sister, brother, parents, aunts, uncles, grandparents, etc.).

|  |  |  |  |
|---|---|---|---|
|  |  |  |  |
|  |  |  |  |
|  |  |  |  |

4. Draw another chart of your own below to fill in details to compare any five things.

|  |  |  |  |
|---|---|---|---|
|  |  |  |  |
|  |  |  |  |
|  |  |  |  |
|  |  |  |  |
|  |  |  |  |

# Can You Picture It?

To remember information easily, link it to a picture you make in your mind or one you draw on paper.

Here is your chance to be an artist, even if you think you can't draw.

Example:
You may need to learn that there are 16 cups, 8 pints and 4 quarts in 1 gallon.

Visualize your picture to learn those facts. If you do, you may never forget it.

Now have *picture perfect fun* making your own memory associations.

1.  Brussels is the capitol of Belgium.  (Hint: Think Brussel sprouts on top of a Belgian waffle.)

2.  Hartford is the capitol of Connecticut.  (Hint: Think connected hearts.)

3.  The meaning of *ajar* is "partly open."  Now you draw a picture that reminds you of *ajar*.

# Amazing Associations

Another way to remember things is to link information to a phrase, sentence, rhyme, or story. You can also think of something familiar to you and relate it to what you are trying to remember.

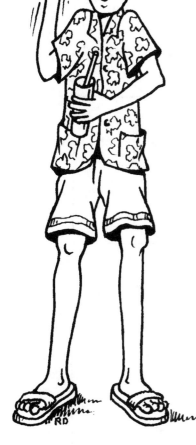

A tall Floridian

Example: Learn some U.S. states and their capitals.
**Tallahassee, Florida**
Tell our Tall Floridian, "Hi."


1. **Springfield, Illinois**
Our association: You can't **spring** out of bed
if you are **ill**.
Your association_____

_____

_____


2. **Augusta, Maine**
Our association: It's **mainly** hot in **August**.
Your association_____

_____

_____


3. **Juno, Alaska**
Our association: It's too cold to go to **Alaska** in **June**.
Your association_____

_____

_____

# Silly Rhymes

Learning songs and rhymes is another easy way to remember facts.  Combine these sayings with a picture, and you have something unforgettable.

6 x 7 = 42

Our silly rhyme: 6 x 7 in a shoe equals 42.

This is our silly picture:

Now its your turn to burst out with a  funky beat and make these *times* a tasty treat!

1.  8 x 8 = 64

Our silly rhyme: 8 x 8 on a door equals 64.
Your silly picture:

2.  7 x 7 = 49

Your silly rhyme:_____
_____

Your silly picture:

3.  6 x 8 = 48

Your silly rhyme_____
_____

Your silly picture:

# I Can Pay Attention TODAY

For some people, paying attention is easy. They have no trouble focusing. For other people, paying attention is harder. They get distracted easily and find it hard to concentrate. Remember when we told you that everyone's brain is different. Some people get tired more easily than others or become bored more quickly. For them paying attention requires greater effort.

On this page and the next two, we have some checklists you can use to see how well you are paying attention. Your teacher may want you to use these in class.

Read each line and circle either "YES" or "NO" to describe how you did in class today.

Date:_____

| | | | |
|---|---|---|---|
| 1. | I paid attention to the teacher today. | YES | NO |
| 2. | I looked at the teacher while a lesson was being taught. | YES | NO |
| 3. | I thought about what was important to remember while the teacher was teaching. | YES | NO |
| 4. | I followed directions I was told. | YES | NO |
| 5. | I read all the directions on written work. | YES | NO |
| 6. | I asked questions if I didn't understand. | YES | NO |
| 7. | I answered a question. | YES | NO |
| 8. | I wrote all my homework in my assignment book. | YES | NO |
| 9. | I remembered to take home what I needed. | YES | NO |
| 10. | I reminded myself to pay attention if I got distracted. | YES | NO |
| 11. | I finished all my work. | YES | NO |

ADD UP THE NUMBER OF TIMES YOU CIRCLED "YES" _____
HOW DID YOU DO?   GREAT   PRETTY GOOD   ROOM FOR IMPROVEMENT
                          9-11         6-10                    1-5

Now it is time to work on the ones you answered "NO." Each week select a new behavior to practice in class. Soon you'll see improvement in your attention and your grades as well.

# I Can Do My Best In Class

Students who are well behaved, and organized often do well in school. Read each line and circle either "YES" or "NO" to describe how you did today in one of the subjects you underline below.

English        Math        Reading        Social Studies        Science

### I CAN PAY ATTENTION
| | | | |
|---|---|---|---|
| 1. | I paid attention to the teacher today | YES | NO |
| 2. | I concentrated on my work and not on other students | YES | NO |
| 3. | I followed directions | YES | NO |
| 4. | I finished all my work | YES | NO |

### I CAN KEEP MY THINGS IN ORDER
| | | | |
|---|---|---|---|
| 5. | My desk was neat | YES | NO |
| 6. | My work was put away in its place | YES | NO |
| 7. | My writing was neat | YES | NO |

### I CAN CONTROL MY BEHAVIOR
| | | | |
|---|---|---|---|
| 8. | I raised my hand | YES | NO |
| 9. | I asked permission before getting up | YES | NO |
| 10. | I cooperated with others | YES | NO |

ADD UP THE NUMBER OF TIMES YOU CIRCLED "YES" _____

HOW DID YOU DO?   GREAT   PRETTY GOOD   ROOM FOR IMPROVEMENT
                         8-10         5-7               1-4

Just as with attention, you can improve your organization and behavior by working on one "NO" answer each week.

# Was I Paying Attention?

## INSTRUCTIONS

Sometimes we need a signal to remind us to pay attention. You can make an audio tape that signals you every one or two minutes. Simply record a "beeping" sound on the tape. Listen to the beep tape as you do your work. Whenever you hear a beep, stop working for a moment and ask yourself, "Was I paying attention?". Mark your answer (√) and go right back to work. Answer the questions on the bottom of the page when you finish.

Was I Paying Attention?

| YES | NO |
|-----|-----|
|  |  |
|  |  |
|  |  |
|  |  |
|  |  |
|  |  |
|  |  |
|  |  |
|  |  |
|  |  |
|  |  |
|  |  |

Was I Paying Attention?

| YES | NO |
|-----|-----|
|  |  |
|  |  |
|  |  |
|  |  |
|  |  |
|  |  |
|  |  |
|  |  |
|  |  |
|  |  |
|  |  |
|  |  |

| | | |
|---|---|---|
| Did I follow the directions? | Yes | No |
| Did I pay attention? | Yes | No |
| Did I finish my work? | Yes | No |
| Did I check my answers? | Yes | No |

* Beep tape available in Listen, Look and Think Program by Harvey C. Parker, Ph.D.

(800) ADD-WARE ©1992 Specialty Press, Inc.

# Chapter 7
# Taking Tests

Teachers use tests to see how much you have learned. Doing well on tests is important if you want to have good grades in school.

In this chapter you will learn strategies to help you earn the best grades on tests. You will learn about five different types of tests that teachers usually give and the strategies you can use to succeed on each type. You will also learn that old tests can help you earn better grades in the future.

Test taking skills.
1. The importance of reading directions carefully.
2. Taking matching tests.
3. Taking true-false tests.
4. Taking fill-in tests.
5. Taking multiple choice tests.
6. Taking essay tests.
7. Making old tests work for you.

# Are You Quick Quiz Qualified?

Are you Quick Quiz Qualified?  Let's test your test taking techniques.
Read the statements and check the box that best applies to you,

AA = Almost Always,   S = Sometimes,   NA = Not Always

| AA | S | NA | |
|----|---|----|---|
| ___ | ___ | ___ | 1.  I write my name on every test paper. |
| ___ | ___ | ___ | 2.  I carefully read and follow directions. |
| ___ | ___ | ___ | 3.  I carefully read the questions and all the answer choices. |
| ___ | ___ | ___ | 4.  I know what to do about the "ringers" on matching tests. |
| ___ | ___ | ___ | 5.  I know which key words to look for on true/false tests that might give me clues. |
| ___ | ___ | ___ | 6.  I know what to do on fill-in-the-blank tests. |
| ___ | ___ | ___ | 7.  I get rid of the impossible answer choices on multiple choice tests and analyze the distracters. |
| ___ | ___ | ___ | 8.  I use my old, graded tests to help prepare for future tests. |

How many AA answers do you have? _____

If you scored:

7-8 You are a terrific test taker who will get even better after you read this chapter.

4-6 You are doing a good job and will learn a lot after reading this chapter.

1-3 We have some terrific test tips that will help you to tackle future tests.

# Today's Test

Directions:  Read all the instructions before you begin this quiz.

1. Write your first name in the top right corner.
2. Underline the word "directions" at the top.
3. Draw a square in the lower left corner of the paper.
4. Write your last name on the bottom right corner.
5. Draw a circle around the page number at the bottom of this page.
6. Draw a star in the top left corner of the page.
7. Draw a happy face near where you wrote your name.
8. Draw hair on the happy face.
9. Draw a body for your happy face.
10. Ignore #1-9 and just write your full name in the upper right corner.


Did you "get" TODAY'S TEST?  Write what you learned about taking tests.

I learned_____

_____

_____

# Matching Tests

Matching tests have two columns of information. You must match the details in one column to the other. For example, you may be required to match a word in column A to its definition in column B, or a place or person with its descriptions.

Here are some tips you should consider when taking a matching test.

1. Write your name on the paper.
2. Read all directions first.
3. Read all of the choices in each column to be aware of possible answers.
4. Beware of the "ringer." If one column has more choices then the other, begin with the shorter column. Why waste time trying to find an answer for a ringer, one with no match.
5. If the teacher lets you write on the test paper, cross out answers as you use them.
6. Look down one of the columns for information you know immediately and match it to the other column. This will reduce the size of the columns one answer at a time with less stress.

# Matching Tests 2

Directions:

1. Match column A with column B.
2. Write the letter choice on the given line.
3. Then use your answers to find the picture by connecting the dots in order from numbers 1 to 9.

Have a good trip!

## KIDS' FOOD FAVORITES

|   A   |   |   B   |
|-------|---|-------|
| ____1. pizza | M | comes from a cow, goes on round bun |
| ____2. hot dog | L | chocolate chip, sugar or oatmeal raisin |
| ____3. spaghetti | T | pop, pop, pop |
| ____4. ice cream | O | I like pepperoni on mine, do you? |
| ____5. hamburger | E | twisted, logs or sticks |
| ____6. french fries | X | great with meatballs and lots of tomato sauce |
| ____7. popcorn | R | long thin potatoes |
| ____8. cookies | N | you can blow big bubbles |
| ____9. gum | H | this food doesn't bark |
|  | J | yummy, cold and served on a cone |

A ·          T·          C·

F ·          D·          G·

L ·          N·          E·

M·          R· ‾O·       H·

B·          I·          K·

        J·          X·

# True or False Tests

This is what you need to know about how to take true-false tests:

1. Write your name on the paper.
2. Read all directions.
3. Read all questions.
4. To be true, the whole statement must be true.
5. Pay attention to *signal* words that teachers include on true/false tests. These signal words are very important, and they can often give you a clue as to whether the sentence is true or false.

   These signal words are often used when a sentence is false.

   | | | |
   |---|---|---|
   | all | every | none |
   | always | only | never |

   These signal words are often used when a sentence is true.

   | | | |
   |---|---|---|
   | some | sometimes | often |
   | usually | probably | except |
   | seldom | mainly | rarely |

6. If you are not sure if a sentence is true or false, answer the other questions and then go back and look at the sentence you were unsure of to answer it later.

# True or False Tests 2

## WHAT ANIMAL IS IT?

Directions: The name of an animal is hiding in the box below. To find it, circle each true or false statement and shade in the shape with that letter.

|  | True | False |
|---|---|---|
| A cat really has nine lives. | R | P |
| Cats come in many sizes and colors. | J | Z |
| A baby cat is called a joey. | M | C |
| A cat always purrs when it is sad. | A | Q |
| Cats sometimes chase mice. | I | W |
| Cats often like to drink milk. | B | U |
| Cats never play with dogs. | E | F |
| Cats often climb on kitchen counters. | S | V |

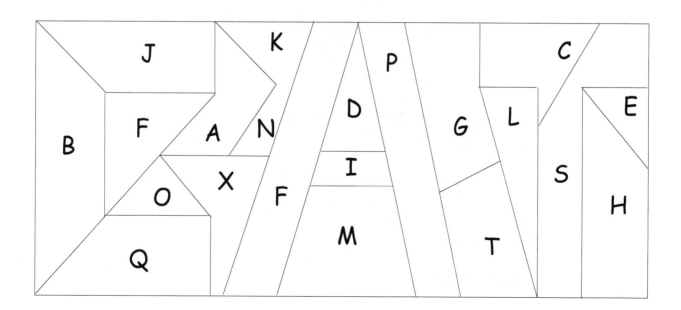

# Fill-in-the-Blanks Tests

Fill-in-the-blank tests require you to memorize details and their explanations or definitions. Then finish a sentence by writing that information in.

1. Write your name on the paper.
2. Read all directions carefully.
3. If there is a word bank, read all of the word choices first.
4. Read the whole sentence. Try to think of the word that you know will fit, and find it in the word bank.
5. Cross off each word in the word bank as you use it.
6. If you don't know an answer, leave it blank. You may find a clue in a later sentence.
7. Reread your answer to make sure it sounds right in the sentence. If it doesn't, it's probably wrong.
8. Don't leave any blanks empty.

# Fill-in-the-Blanks Tests 2

**Directions:**

These sentences are all about musical instruments. Read each sentence and fill in each blank with an answer from the word bank. Use your answers to fill in the crossword puzzle.

| conductor | guitar | cymbals | triangle | violin |
|-----------|--------|---------|----------|--------|
| drum | piano | flute | notes | |

**Across**

1 The _____ is not only an instrument, it's a shape, too.

2 The four-stringed _____ is often the star of the orchestra.

3 Beating sticks on a big _____ can make a loud booming sound.

4 Metal discs clanged together are _____ .

5 Musicians read _____ to play music.

**Down**

6 The _____ leads a band or orchestra with a stick called a baton.

7 You hold this pipe-shaped metal instrument to your lips sideways and gently blow.

8 As fingers tap white and black keys, a _____ makes a melodious sound.

9 Singers like to strum the strings of their _____ .

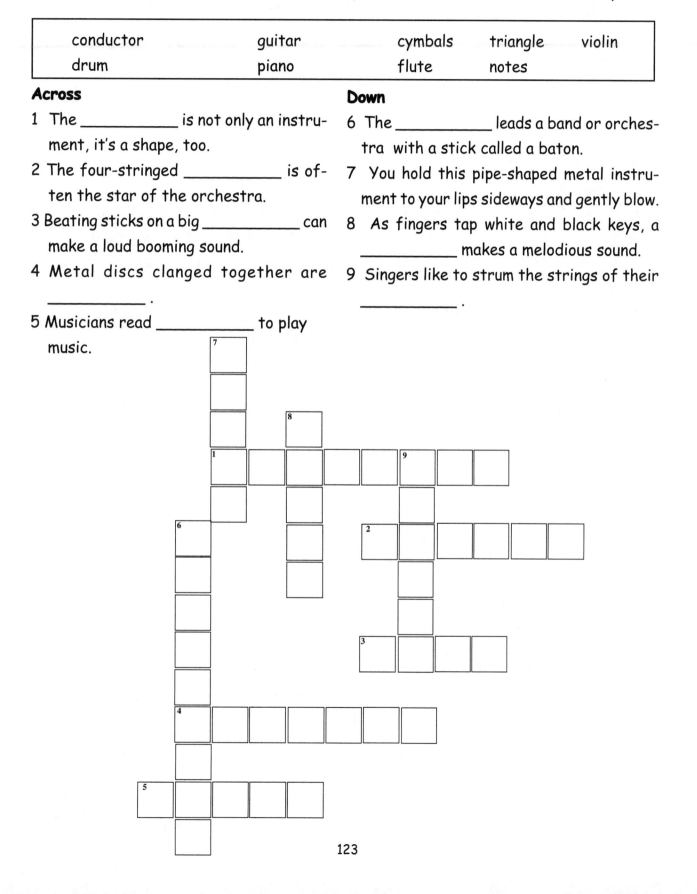

# Multiple Choice Tests

On multiple choice tests, the answer is actually given. All you need to do is recognize the correct answer from the given choices.

These strategies will help you do well on multiple choice tests.

1. Write your name on the paper.
2. Read the directions carefully.
3. Read each question carefully.
4. Read all the answer choices and cross out the ones you know are wrong .
5. After you have crossed out the answers that you are sure are wrong, read the ones that are left. Reread the question carefully and decide which answer is the best choice.
6. Look out for the distracters! Distracters are answers that are almost correct but do not answer the question completely.
7. If you are unsure of the answer, choose among the remaining choices.

# Multiple Choice Tests 2

# SPORTS MANIA

Directions:

Read the following statements and circle the correct answer.  Write the letter you choose above the question number in the blank spaces on the next page.  (If you are not a sports fan, ask for help from someone who is.)

1. The National Hockey League champions win
    D       the Orange Bowl
    R       the Stanley Cup
    N       the World Cup
    Q       the Tootsie Roll

2. People who enter the Tour de France
    Z       play tennis
    V       climb the Eiffel Tower
    E       ride bicycles
    B       lift weights

3. These games, held both summer and winter, bring together athletes from countries around the world.
    F       the U.S. Open
    K       the Spring Games
    A       the Olympic Games
    D       the Asian Games

4. What sport does one play in order to win the green jacket at the Masters?
    S       golf
    B       tennis
    J       softball
    W       soccer

5.  What game is played during March Madness?
    V       football
    L       baseball
    X       soccer
    O       basketball

6.  Which event determines the National Football League's championship team?
    M       the Rose Bowl
    C       the Cotton Bowl
    T       the Super Bowl
    D       the Best Bowl

7.  In baseball, what does RBI stand for?
    L       runs by inches
    H       reds bat incomplete
    U       runs batted in
    F       Risky Business, Inc.

8.  What major soccer tournament is held every four years?
    G       the American Cup
    M       the Coffee Cup
    X       the Stanley Cup
    P       the World Cup

9.  In what game is "love" a score?
    Y       tennis
    I       basketball
    J       volleyball
    C       figure skating

Fill in the blanks below and read the sentence you have just written.

__ __ __   __ __ __ __   __ __ __ __ __   __ __ __ __ __
9  5  7   3  1  2  3   4  7  8  2  1   4  8  5  1  6

# Learning From Old Tests

If you get a disappointing grade on a test, don't throw the test away. You can learn a lot from your mistakes. Use a disappointing test grade to find out what changes you need to make so that you can do better next time. Read the following questions about your disappointing test and circle Yes or No.

| | | | |
|---|---|---|---|
| Yes | No | 1. | I carefully read the textbook using the "Helpful Hamburger". |
| Yes | No | 2. | I used "Facts Layer by Layer" to take notes of the most important facts. |
| Yes | No | 3. | I used the "Inside Scoop" to make study questions of the most important information. |
| Yes | No | 4. | I reviewed my notes and study questions. |
| Yes | No | 5. | When studying, someone asked my study questions to me out loud. |
| Yes | No | 6. | When studying, I read my study questions. |
| Yes | No | 7. | I answered the study questions out loud. |
| Yes | No | 8. | I answered the study questions by writing down the answers. |
| Yes | No | 9. | I used some of the "Memory Magic" to learn the facts. |
| Yes | No | 10. | Before starting the test, I carefully read and understood the directions. |
| Yes | No | 11. | While taking the test, I carefully read and understood the questions. |
| Yes | No | 12. | I remembered the facts I studied while taking the test. |
| Yes | No | 13. | I am happy with the grade I received on this test. |

What changes can you make to do better on your next text?

_____

_____

_____

# Internet Homework Resources

The following Internet sites were active at the time of publication of this resource list.  These Internet sites offer ideas for science projects, art projects, and can provide help with organization, and information for reports.  Since Internet sites change frequently, these sites may not be operating when you check them.

www.familyeducation .com
www.worldvillage.com
www.elishomeworkhelp.com
www.wiltonlibrary.org
www.awesomelibrary.org
www.yahooligans.com

# Answer Key

Page 41 — Double-Checking Math Work
Problems containing mistakes and their correct answers.

1. 66      6. 8
3. 56      8. 55 cents
4. 85      9. $1.33
5. 39     12. 2808

Page 44 — Picture Perfect Understanding  1) B  2) C  3) A, B

Page 46 — 1) fishing  2) The boy is trying to catch the big fish.  3) The boy hooked the fish. The fish is trying to get away.

Page 47 — 1) a birthday party.  2) The boy had a birthday party with a birthday cake and presents.  3) happy birthday banner, birthday cake and candles, presents, other children  4) A boy had a birthday party with a birthday cake, presents, and other children to help him celebrate.

Page 48 — 1) Sally's bathroom  2) Sally's bathroom is decorated in an ocean theme.  3) The tiles look like waves. The shower curtain is painted with plants. The floor mats have sewn shells and seahorse decals are on the mirrors.

Page 49 — 1) dragons  2) Dragons are not real.  3) Long ago people believed that dragons were real. There were many stories about knights fighting the dragons but no proof they ever lived.

Page 50 — 1) a shipwreked man.  2) Gulliver had many adventures when he was shipwrecked.  3) His first adventure was with the tiny Lilliputians. Next he went to Brobdingnag where the people were very tall. Gulliver was the main character in Gulliver's Travels.

Page 52 — Topic: my sister, the bookworm
        Main Idea: My sister is a bookworm because she loves to read.
        Details: There are books all over her room. She is always reading. She reads under the covers with a flashlight.

Page 53 — Topic: Central Park
        Main Idea: Central Park is a wonderful place to spend a spring day.
        Details: People skate, roller blade and skateboard. Others play instruments or listen to musicians. People visit the Central Park Zoo.

Page 56 — Topic: sleeping
        Main Idea: People sleep in different places.
        Details: most people sleep on mattresses. Some sleep in sleeping bags and others sleep on floor mats.

Page 57 — Topic: a Florida vacation
        Main Idea: A Florida vacation includes many choices besides Disney World.
        Details: St. Augustine is Florida's oldest city. Florida's panhandle has beautiful beaches. Visit Miami and the Florida Keys to fish, swim, and meet people from all around the world.

Page 59 — Topic: Carl the parrot
        Paragraph 1

Main Idea: Betsy is unhappy about her sister Melinda's pet parrot, Carl.
Details: Carl's talking keeps Betsy up at night. He is a sloppy eater. Betsy is allergic
to Carl's feathers.
Paragraph 2
Main Idea: Betsy's feelings about Carl change.
Details: Carl's claw was stuck between the metal bars. Melinda was able to release
Carl. Carl flies on Melinda's shoulder and they become friends.

Page 81 — Topic: The True Story of the Three Pigs!
Paragraph 1
Main Idea: The story, The Three Little Pigs, is wrong according to A. Wolf.
Details: A. Wolf never meant to kill the pigs or blow their houses down.
The pigs were not smart. The wolf had a cold.
Paragraph 2
Main Idea: A. Wolf tells his story.
Details: Wolf goes to borrow sugar from the pigs. He blew down the first two pigs'
houses because he had a cold and sneezed. The third pig called the police.

Page 73 — See page 77

Page 75 — See page 78

Page 106 — Charming Charts
Compare baseball, football and basketball.

|  | # of players | Quarters/ Innings | Played on a....... | Size or shape of ball |
|---|---|---|---|---|
| Baseball | 9 | innings | diamond | round |
| Football | 11 | quarters | field | spherical |
| Basketball | 5 | quarters | court | round |

Page 119 — Matching Tests 2
1. O          6. R
2. H          7. T
3. X          8. L
4. J          9. N
5. M

Page 121 — True or False Tests 2
P, J, C, Q, I, B, F, S

Page 123 — Fill-in-the-Blanks Test 2
1. triangle          6. conductor
2. violin            7. flute
3. drum              8. piano
4. cymbals           9. guitar
5. notes

Page 125 — Multiple Choice Tests 2
1. R          6. T
2. E          7. U
3. A          8. P
4. S          9. Y
5. O

# Forms You May Copy

Grade Chart
Get It Done Today!
Today's Homework Assignment Planner
Monthly Planner
Reading Comprehension Workshop
Mind Mapping
My Dictionary
Note Your Facts Layer by Layer
Chapter Map
Was I Paying Attention

# GRADE CHART

KEY:
T = test   Q = quiz
HW= homework
P= project

| COURSE | WEEK #  1 | 2 | 3 | 4 | 5 | 6 | 7 | 8 | 9 | Report Card Grade |
|---|---|---|---|---|---|---|---|---|---|---|
| Grade I want ___ | | | | | | | | | | |
| Grade I want ___ | | | | | | | | | | |
| Grade I want ___ | | | | | | | | | | |
| Grade I want ___ | | | | | | | | | | |
| Grade I want ___ | | | | | | | | | | |

# Get It Done Today!

Date: _____

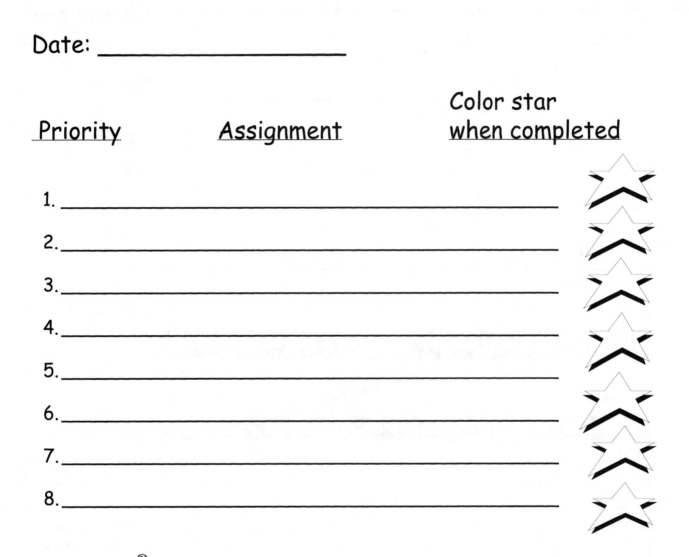

| Priority | Assignment | Color star when completed |
|----------|------------|---------------------------|
| 1. _____ | | ⭐ |
| 2. _____ | | ⭐ |
| 3. _____ | | ⭐ |
| 4. _____ | | ⭐ |
| 5. _____ | | ⭐ |
| 6. _____ | | ⭐ |
| 7. _____ | | ⭐ |
| 8. _____ | | ⭐ |

Tip

After you know how to plan, use this shortcut. Use your homework planner to prioritize your work by writing "1" next to the assignment to be done first, "2" next to the one to be done second and so forth.

# Today's Homework Assignment Planner

Name: _____  Day: _____  Date: _____

| Priority | Subjects | Homework Assignments | Due | Supplies Needed |
|---|---|---|---|---|
| | **Language Arts** | | | |
| | **Math** | | | |
| | **Reading** | | | |
| | **Spelling** | | | |
| | | | | |
| | | | | |

**Are all assignments copied?** Yes No **Teacher's initials:** _____

Name: _____  Day: _____  Date: _____

| Priority | Subjects | Homework Assignments | Due | Supplies Needed |
|---|---|---|---|---|
| | **Language Arts** | | | |
| | **Math** | | | |
| | **Reading** | | | |
| | **Spelling** | | | |
| | | | | |
| | | | | |

**Are all assignments copied?** Yes No **Teacher's initials:** _____

# Monthly Planner

A monthly planner will help you keep track of important dates. Record important dates such as when tests will be given, when projects are due, field trips, etc.

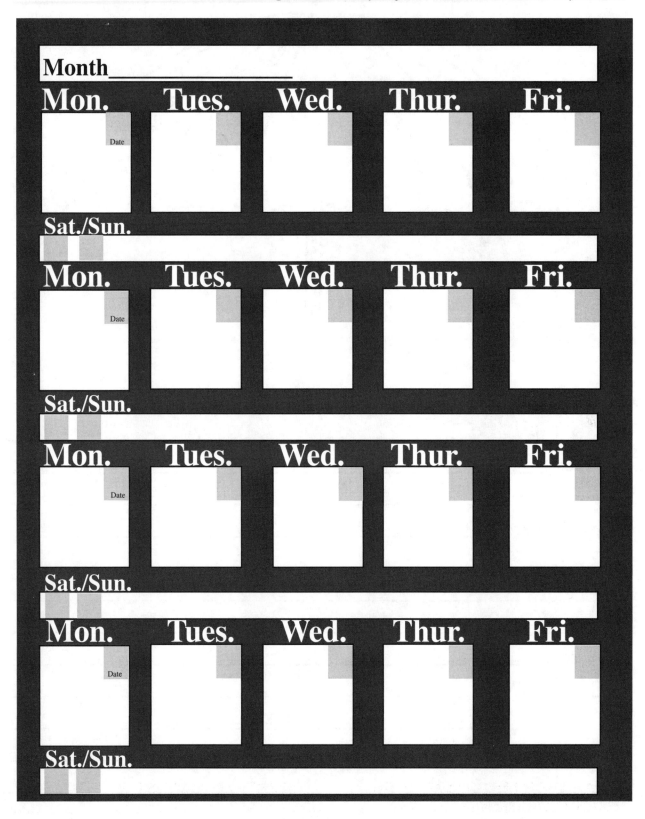

**Month**_____

| **Mon.** | **Tues.** | **Wed.** | **Thur.** | **Fri.** |
| --- | --- | --- | --- | --- |
| Date | | | | |

**Sat./Sun.**

| **Mon.** | **Tues.** | **Wed.** | **Thur.** | **Fri.** |
| --- | --- | --- | --- | --- |
| Date | | | | |

**Sat./Sun.**

| **Mon.** | **Tues.** | **Wed.** | **Thur.** | **Fri.** |
| --- | --- | --- | --- | --- |
| Date | | | | |

**Sat./Sun.**

| **Mon.** | **Tues.** | **Wed.** | **Thur.** | **Fri.** |
| --- | --- | --- | --- | --- |
| Date | | | | |

**Sat./Sun.**

# Reading Comprehension Worksheet

# Main Idea

SUPPORTING DETAILS
SUPPORTING DETAILS
SUPPORTING DETAILS
SUPPORTING DETAILS
SUPPORTING DETAILS

PARAPHRASE

Topic or Title: _____

Main idea: _____

_____

Supporting details: _____

_____

_____

Paraphrase: _____

_____

_____

_____

_____

# Mind Mapping

Title of book _____Author_____

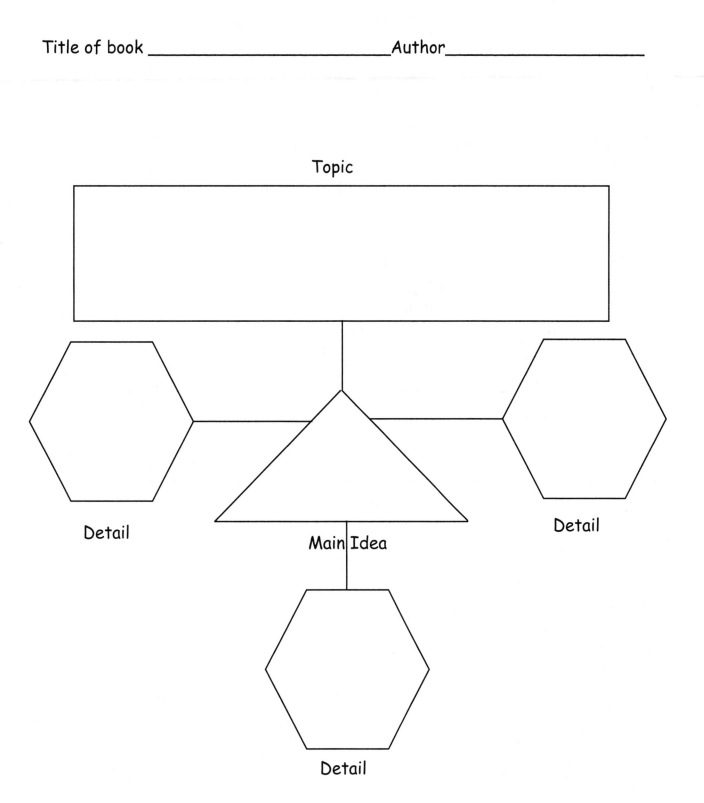

Topic

Detail

Detail

Main Idea

Detail

# Mind Mapping

Title of book _____ Author_____

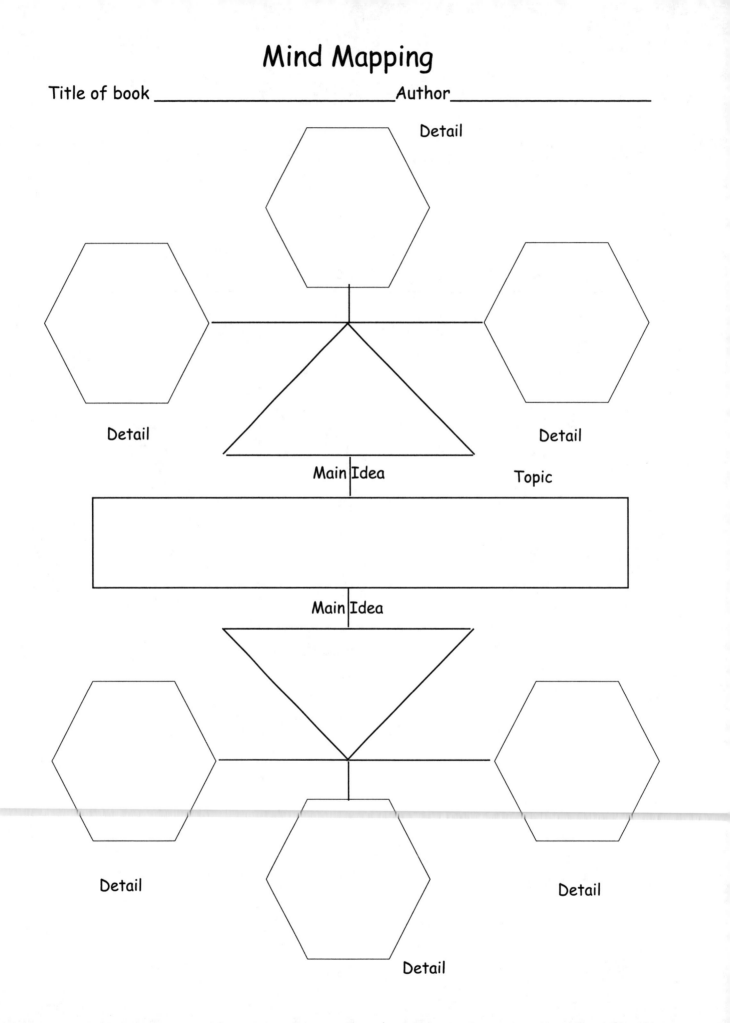

Detail

Detail

Detail

Main Idea

Topic

Main Idea

Detail

Detail

Detail

# MY DICTIONARY

| WORD | MEANING | SENTENCE | PERSONAL CLUE* |
|---|---|---|---|
| | | | |
| | | | |

* A word part or picture to help you remember.

# Note Your Facts Layer by Layer

Write the important facts of a story to build your layer cake below.

1. Write the title of the story.

   _____

2. Write the main idea of paragraph #1.

   _____

   _____

   _____

3. Write the details that support the main idea of paragraph # 1.

   SD1:_____

   SD2:_____

   SD3:_____

4. Write the main idea of paragraph #2.

   _____

   _____

5. Write the details that support the main idea of paragraph # 2.

   SD 1: _____

   SD 2: _____

   SD 3: _____

2. Write the main idea of paragraph #3.

   _____

   _____

3. Write the details that support the main idea of paragraph # 3.

   SD 1: _____

   SD 2: _____

   SD 3: _____

# Chapter Map

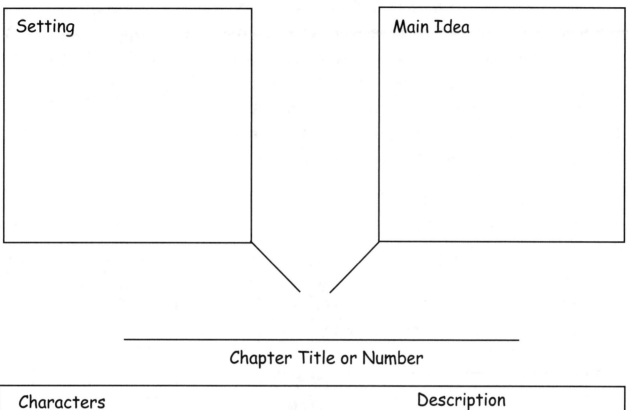

Setting

Main Idea

_____

Chapter Title or Number

| Characters | Description |
|---|---|
|  |  |
|  |  |
|  |  |
|  |  |

Important facts to remember

# "Was I Paying Attention?" Form

## INSTRUCTIONS

You can make an audio tape that signals you every one or two minutes. Simply record a "beeping" sound on the tape. Listen to the beep tape as you do your work. Whenever you hear a beep, stop working for a moment and ask yourself, "Was I paying attention?". Mark your answer (√) and go right back to work. Answer the questions on the bottom of the page when you finish.

Was I Paying Attention?

| YES | NO |
|-----|-----|
|     |     |
|     |     |
|     |     |
|     |     |
|     |     |
|     |     |
|     |     |
|     |     |
|     |     |
|     |     |
|     |     |
|     |     |
|     |     |
|     |     |
|     |     |

Was I Paying Attention?

| YES | NO |
|-----|-----|
|     |     |
|     |     |
|     |     |
|     |     |
|     |     |
|     |     |
|     |     |
|     |     |
|     |     |
|     |     |
|     |     |
|     |     |
|     |     |
|     |     |
|     |     |

| | | |
|---|---|---|
| Did I follow the directions? | Yes | No |
| Did I pay attention? | Yes | No |
| Did I finish my work? | Yes | No |
| Did I check my answers? | Yes | No |

* Beep tape available in Listen, Look and Think Program by Harvey C. Parker, Ph.D.
(800) ADD-WARE ©1992 Specialty Press, Inc.